LOVE YO

also by Mike James

FATAL ATTRACTION
ON DEATH ROW
WOMEN ON DEATH ROW
BEDSIDE BOOK OF MURDER

LOVE YOU TO DEATH

Compiled by Mike James

TRUE
CRIME
LIBRARY

True Crime Library
A Forum Press Book
by the Paperback Division of
Forum Design,
P.O. Box 157, London SE20 7QA

An Imprint of True Crime Library
© 1995 Forum Design
All rights reserved

Editorial team:
Tristan Ashman & Anna Bennett
12 Flitcroft Street, London WC2

Typeset by Techniset,
1 Back Cross Lane, Newton-le-Willows,
Merseyside, WA12 9YE.
Printed and bound in Great Britain by
Harper Collins Manufacturing, Glasgow

ISBN 1 874358 08 7

CONTENTS

FOREWORD

by Colin Wilson

At the time this book was being compiled, the British press was going through one of its periodic bouts of moral indignation – this time about whether true crime stories should be presented on television and radio. As a result of this furore, the director Michael Winner was reported to have cancelled another series of true crime programmes. BBC television even experienced doubts about its Crimewatch programme, designed to help catch criminals, while its presenter, Nick Ross, changed his mind about writing an introduction to a book called *Murder Most Foul*, based on his own radio series and written by my sons Damon and Rowan. The argument, as far as I could make out, was that programmes about true crime encouraged criminals to go out and imitate them.

This, of course, is total nonsense. Books on crime have been popular ever since The Newgate Calendar appeared in 1774, and as far as I know, no one has ever been inspired to go out and commit a murder by reading about it – although it is true that some murderers have had a taste for crime books; in the early 1960s, a man named William MacDonald killed and sexually mutilated a number of men in Sydney, Australia, and when arrested, was found to be in possession of my *Encyclopedia of Murder* and my Jack the Ripper novel, *Ritual in the Dark*. Asked by a detective why he wanted to read such rubbish, he explained: "It's the only thing I get any pleasure from." But investigation of MacDonald's background revealed that he had possessed sadistic tendencies long before he read my books. He read these books because he possessed sadistic tendencies, so cause and effect were the other way round.

In fact, MacDonald's medical history gives us a clear idea of how such criminals develop. An active homosexual who solicited in toilets, he moved from job to job in England because his obvious homosexuality led to persecution at work. After a nervous breakdown – during which he heard voices – he moved to Australia hoping to lead a quiet life; but things were just as bad there, and again he was driven from job to job. Hatred and violence built up in him until when he was drinking one day in the room of a friend, he was suddenly overwhelmed by an urge to strangle the other man. After the murder, MacDonald left the body tucked up in bed and left. For days he was terrified of arrest; then, to his amazement, he saw in a newspaper that the death had been diagnosed as accidental. Enormous relief was followed by the realisation that the murder had satisfied some deep urge to violence. From then on, he began to pick up derelicts, got them drunk, then stabbed them to death and mutilated their genitals.

Apart from these strange periods of violence, MacDonald was a normal human being. He even made a success of a small shop which he bought. Then one night the urge overcame him and he killed another drinking companion in his living room, stabbing him repeatedly until the floor and walls were covered in blood. The next day he buried the man under the floor, and then fled. When the body was found, it was so badly decomposed that it was mistaken for MacDonald himself. Six months later, when a man who knew him saw the "dead" MacDonald walking down the street, he told the police. The body was exhumed, and identified by the fingerprints as a petty thief named Hackett. A manhunt led to

MacDonald's arrest and a life sentence, with the recommendation that he should never be released.

What the case teaches us is that MacDonald became a serial killer out of a mixture of resentment and guilt. In the more tolerant atmosphere of our own time, he would never have become a killer because his homosexuality would have been accepted. And that, I submit, is an excellent argument for a more "open" society, where problematic issues are openly discussed.

The first case in this book underlines the same point. Alberto DeSalvo, the Boston Strangler, was what is known to psychiatrists as a "satyr", someone whose sexual urge is violent and uncontrollable; his wife complained that he needed sex on average half a dozen times a day. As the "Measuring Man", he persuaded women he worked for a modelling agency, and asked to take their measurements. He never attempted assault – although some of the women, hoping for a job, gave themselves voluntarily – or even any kind of familiarity. Arrested when loitering in a garden, he was sentenced to two years' imprisonment, and told the prison authorities that he thought there was something wrong with him and he needed treatment. They ignored him and he was released. Out of prison, after two years of frustration, he soon graduated to rape, then to murder. At first he strangled his victims; but when he killed Beverley Sams with a knife, he felt a compulsion to keep on stabbing her repeatedly, the same compulsion that had driven MacDonald. (This repeated stabbing is a psychological oddity often found in serial killers.)

Eventually caught through his own confession in prison, DeSalvo went on begging for psychological treatment and was still ignored. Perhaps the prison authorities felt there was no point in trying to "cure" a man who was in prison for life. If so, they showed the same hopeless short-sightedness that led them to ignore his pleas for help when he was in prison as the "Measuring Man." If they had listened to him then, he would not have become the Boston Strangler. Why didn't they listen to him? Because there was not enough public awareness of people like DeSalvo and their problems.

Thirty years later, that is certainly no longer true. DeSalvo was one of the first of the epidemic of so-called "serial killers" (the term invented in the late 1970s by FBI agent Robert Rossler), and was followed by others like Ian Brady, Dean Corll, John Gacy, the "Hillside Stranglers" Buono and Bianchi, Dennis Nilsen, Henry Lee Lucas and Leonard Lake. The FBI began to study them at its "psychological profiling" unit at Quantico, Virginia, and the newspapers began to write about them, sometimes wildly overestimating the number of serial killers who were still uncaught and operating "out there." (The estimate varied from a thousand to fifty – but the latter figure is closer to the truth.) Novelists like Thomas Harris, Philip Kerr and Patricia Cornwell took up the theme, and the film version of *Silence of the Lambs* suddenly made even the most sheltered individuals aware of what was happening.

I have to confess that I have always found something slightly distasteful in this fictionalising of serial murder. Although my own *Ritual in the Dark* was based on Peter Kürten (who will be found in the present volume), my interest was in the psychology of the killer. The modern serial-crime novel is shamelessly unrealistic – the serial killer Dennis Nilsen went to the heart of the matter when he complained that Harris's Hannibal Lecter is not in the least like a real serial murderer, because Harris represents him as potent and demonic, while most serial killers feel impotent and vulnerable, which is precisely why they kill. But then, it could be argued that *Silence of the Lambs* is just a gruesome modern fairy tale, like those tales of ogres and Bluebeards that made us shudder as children. I suspect that, in spite of the nastiness that I find off-putting, such books actually do little harm.

I have to follow this with the admission that there are rare exceptions. One of them can be found in this volume in the chapter called "The Cannibal of Paris." When I was in Tokyo a few years ago, signing books, the man at the front of the queue asked me to sign one "To Issei Sagawa." He was, indeed, the man who had shot and then partly eaten a Dutch student, Renée Hartevelt, and been released after two years and allowed to return to Japan. We became friendly and corresponded, and when I asked to write about him, he was totally frank about the murder and its aftermath.

I then learned what had turned Sagawa into a cannibal. As a child he was undersized and shy. At birthday parties, his father and an uncle used to play a game in which his father was a brave knight and the uncle was a wicked giant who ate children. The uncle would snatch up Issei and his brother and carry them off to his cooking pot; the father, who tried to rescue them, would get killed by the ogre. Issei, who was prone to daydream and fantasise, was morbidly obsessed by this idea of being eaten; even at the age of three it gave him an odd masochistic thrill. Later, when he turned into a shy and undersized teenager, his sexual daydreams were not simply of seducing some beautiful western film star like Grace Kelly (his obsession was with white women) but of then eating her. (The Japanese, of course, love raw fish, and even some raw meat.) He was so worried about this that he rang a doctor to ask his advice, but the doctor refused to talk over the telephone and asked him to come to his surgery; Sagawa was too ashamed. In his late teens he climbed into the bedroom of a western woman to attack her; she screamed and he was arrested. And still his admission of his sexual problems to a doctor failed to arouse any interest. By the time he went to Paris, he was obsessed by the feeling: "If I don't taste female flesh now, I never shall." Yet as soon as he had killed Renée Hartevelt and carried out the fantasy, it burst like a bubble, leaving him feeling as if he had awakened from a nightmare. Nowadays, making a living from books and journalism, and about to get married, he admits that the idea of cannibalism retains a certain emotional fascination – as all deep-seated fantasies do – but after experiencing the real thing, the old morbid compulsion has evaporated.

Again we see that it was Sagawa's loneliness, his inability to communicate that led to murder. If such things had been widely known – as they are now, due largely to Sagawa's book – Renée Hartevelt would still be alive.

To argue that we should pretend such things do not exist is like arguing we should ignore Aids, instead of openly admitting its existence and trying to prevent it.

So where writing and reading about murder is concerned, I am impenitent. All communication is healthy. It is repression and silence that leads to stagnation, and breeds what Blake called "reptiles of the mind".

Colin Wilson

1

ALBERTO DESALVO: THE BOSTON STRANGLER

Alberto DeSalvo's sexual appetite was extraordinary. He thought about sex night and day. He was married to an attractive German girl, Irmgard, who was certainly no prude. But DeSalvo's sex drive was far too much for her. "Five or six times a day don't mean much to me," he said, thus explaining his wife's permanent state of exhaustion.

In comparison to what happened later, DeSalvo's first sex crimes were little more than games. He would approach young, attractive women in their apartments and tell them he represented a modelling agency. He told his victims that they had been selected as possible candidates for modelling assignments on television, and fame and fortune beckoned.

Hundreds of hopeful young women opened their doors to the charming trickster and DeSalvo, clipboard and tape measure in hand, would measure their vital statistics. He did not necessarily make overt sexual approaches, but he did seduce a good number of these prospective candidates. He later claimed that many of the would-be models seduced him too.

Though they did receive a good number of complaints, the police were not overly concerned by these antics, and it took nearly two years for their so-called "Measuring Man" to be brought to justice. But DeSalvo duly appeared in court at last, and was sentenced to two years behind bars.

DeSalvo was released in the spring of 1961 and returned to his wife and family. But he was a changed man. The experience of prison had hardened him and made him far more ruthless. No more would he use the innocent ruse of measuring his victims. Now he would beat them and tie them up. In the months that followed he waged a campaign of rape and burglary throughout New England. He later bragged that he tied up and raped six women in one morning. He put the total number at more than 1,000.

It was in June 1962 that DeSalvo began to add murder to his methods. His first victim was 55-year-old Anna Slesers, whose naked body was found spreadeagled on the floor of her apartment. He had used a cord to strangle her, and, in an artistic flourish that was to become his trademark, tied the ends together in a jaunty bow.

Within two weeks he had struck again. His next victim was 85-year-old Mary Mullen. On June 30th, 1962, he made his third killing, Helen Blake, a 65-year-old nurse. Next was Nina Nichols, another woman in her sixties. On August 19th, 1962, DeSalvo raped and strangled 75-year-old Ida Irga. Then it was the turn of Jane Sullivan, 67.

After the Sullivan killing there was a short pause in DeSalvo's murderous activities. But then, on December 5th, 1962, they recommenced. This time the victim was slightly closer to the killer's age. She was 25-year-old Sophie Clark, a tall, attractive black woman. DeSalvo had gained entrance into her apartment using the same trick he had employed as the Measuring Man. This time, however, it was a cord and not a measuring tape that served as his weapon. He raped Clark and then strangled her, leaving her naked body, legs spreadeagled, on the bed. The telltale tied bow was beneath the cord he had used to strangle her.

Three days later 23-year-old Patricia Bissette met the same fate, this time strangled with her own stockings.

On February 16th, DeSalvo selected a ninth victim. This time, however, he did not enjoy success. The woman hit him and beat him and screamed for help. DeSalvo fled her apartment like a startled rabbit.

This failure may explain why on his next attack DeSalvo once again chose an older woman. It might also explain why this attack was so uncharacteristically vicious. DeSalvo was carrying a length of lead pipe when he called on the home of 69-year-old Mary Brown, and he used it to smash her head to a pulp. When he raped the poor woman she was already dead. Afterwards he drove a fork into her breast, leaving it embedded in the flesh. Then, perversely, DeSalvo strangled the corpse.

Pretty Beverley Sams, a 23-year-old student at Cambridge, Massachusetts, was at home on the evening of May 6th, 1963, when an intruder burst into her apartment. He tied her to the bed and then raped her repeatedly. He used the girl's stockings to strangle her, but then he took out his knife and began to stab her. "Once I stabbed her, I couldn't stop," he later confessed. "I kept hitting her and hitting her with the knife... I hit her and hit her and hit her." The autopsy revealed twenty-two separate wounds.

The public were now close to panic as they heard more and more about the monster that was evidently in their midst. The police seemed powerless. They set up a special "Strangler Bureau" to collect information, but it got them nowhere. Many sexual deviants were questioned, and a good number of confessions were made. But DeSalvo remained on the loose. On September 8th, 1963, he struck again, raping and strangling 58-year-old Evelyn Crobin. Two months later, on November 23rd, the discovery of 23-year-old Joan Graff's naked body told the police that there was now a twelfth victim. And then, on January 4th, 1964, the Boston Strangler killed again.

Nineteen-year-old Mary Sullivan was raped and strangled in her apartment. Bizarrely, before he left, DeSalvo inserted a broom into her vagina and placed a card between her toes which read "Happy New Year."

For ten months after this last killing, there were no more murders, and the police and public speculated hopefully that the Strangler's reign had come to an end. On October 27th, however, DeSalvo struck again.

A woman reported being attacked in her home by an intruder who matched the description of the "Measuring Man". He pinned her down to the bed and threatened her with a knife. "Don't make a sound or I'll kill you," he told her. The woman, however, managed to fight her attacker off and he fled into the night. She later made a full report of the incident to the police.

Alberto DeSalvo was arrested shortly afterwards. He confessed to two rapes and over four hundred burglaries, and was sent to the Boston State Hospital for observation. It was whilst he was in the hospital that he admitted to being the Strangler, even confessing to two more killings to add to the known murder count of thirteen.

Quizzed by detectives, DeSalvo revealed many facts about the crimes that had been kept secret from the public and the press. After a short while they were left in no doubt that he was indeed the Boston Strangler.

Ironically, however, Alberto DeSalvo was never charged with the crime. Instead he came to court facing four charges of rape. Sentenced to life imprisonment in 1967, DeSalvo was stabbed to death by a fellow prisoner on November 26th, 1973.

2

BEHEADED IN THE BATH

As the sun came up over the great sprawling city of Buenos Aires on February 18th, 1955, a night watchman was out walking his little dog. As he passed a corner of Avenidas Marquez and Antartida Argentina he caught sight of a large, neatly wrapped package partly concealed in a drain. His dog sniffed the bundle and began to yelp frantically. The man bent down and examined it. He ripped open a corner of the brown paper and pushed aside the inner wrapping of blue and white striped plastic. Then he staggered back. He had uncovered a woman's torso.

Later, at police headquarters, the grisly bundle was examined. The torso was that of a fair-skinned woman. She had been about 5 feet 2 inches tall and between 20 and 30 years old. She had been slim and shapely and probably attractive, but there was no real way to know. Her head had been removed so too had her limbs. There was no means of identification.

One week later a young housewife was walking home from the grocery store, with her two little daughters. Her path took her past a water-filled ditch beside a malodorous garbage dump. Suddenly the woman stopped in her tracks and drew her two little girls close to her. Protruding from the ditch's dirty water were two human feet.

Policemen retrieved the two legs; they also found a

single thigh. These were taken to headquarters and fitted to the unidentified torso. They were a match. Unfortunately, however, they provided no clue except that the dead woman had frequently visited a chiropodist.

That same day, at 5 o'clock in the afternoon. a young sailor caught sight of a wire rubbish basket, crammed to the brim and floating in the oily, dirty water of the harbour. He called a policeman and the two men fished it out with long poles. In the basket were the head and arms of the murdered woman. The head by now was quite unrecognizable. Fingerprinting too was impossible; the murderer had removed the fingertips.

All was not lost, however, for X-rays of the corpse's teeth turned up the best clue to date: an extra tooth, hidden under the gums near the jawbone. Only one person in 100,000 has such a tooth, and in due course the police managed to use this information to make an identification: the unfortunate victim was a 25-year-old woman by the name of Alcira Metygher.

Within a few hours a search for Alcira's family brought detectives to her younger sister, Aña. She told them that she had not seen Alcira for some time, since she had been working away from home. She knew, however, that her sister had two sweethearts, neither of whom knew the other existed. She had seen one of them recently, she said. His name was Jorge Burgos.

Police went to Burgos' house and knocked on the door. An elderly woman answered. Yes, she said, she was Señora Burgos and she had a son named Jorge. Why did they want to know?

"Señora, do you recognise this plastic tablecloth?" The detective showed her the blue-and-white striped material in which Alcira's torso had been wrapped.

"Why, that's mine! I knew that cleaning woman had stolen it! But I didn't go to the police about it. How did you get it?" the woman exclaimed breathlessly. The officer gave no reply.

Señora Burgos was then asked to tell the officers where her son could be found. After speaking to her husband she told them that Jorge had caught a train to the resort of Mar del Plata. She gave the detectives the details of her son's ticket and his seat.

As the officers left the couple looked at one another apprehensively. There were so many rumours of an uprising against Peron, so many arrests every day. Had Jorge been dabbling in politics? They hoped it was nothing like that.

Jorge Eduardo Burgos, an inconspicuous plump little man, was picked up later that day.

"You are under arrest," an officer said.

Burgos stared at them, surprised, but quite unruffled. "You are wrong," he replied. "I didn't kill Alcira. You are making a terrible mistake."

There was a mistake, the detective reasoned, a very obvious one. But it had not been his own. It was Burgos'. No one had levelled a charge against him. No one had mentioned Alcira's name. Burgos had therefore condemned himself with his own denial.

The killer was taken to the police headquarters in Buenos Aires, where his initial calmness quickly evaporated. He fell apart completely in a frenzy of hysteria as he was led into the office. Shortly afterwards he confessed his crime.

"Yes, I killed her," he said. "And I cut her up, too. She was making a fool of me and I was blind with jealousy."

Once Burgos began to talk he spilled everything. Police often had to slow him down so the stenographer could keep up with him. "She kept me on a string for more than four years," he said. "She got lots of money from me, for clothes and beauty parlours, but when I made advances to her, even when I asked her to marry me, she laughed in my face.

"That day – it was February 17th – was the first time she was as generous with me as she had been with others.

But while she was out of the room I found a letter to her between the pages of a book she was reading. It was a love letter all about 'eternal love,' and was signed 'Pascual.' That proved she'd been unfaithful to me.

"We fought. She bit my finger, she kicked me, she scratched me. I was so angry I didn't know what I was doing. I took her by the throat and squeezed, harder and harder. She fainted. I put her on the bed and went out for a walk to calm down.

"About an hour and half later I came back. I hoped to find Alcira feeling better and that she'd be sorry. I thought I'd go mad when I found she was dead. Then I thought of my family, my mother and father and my 11-year-old little sister. How awful it would be if they knew I'd brought a woman to the house while they were away. And there she was, dead. I didn't know what to do. I was so tired and bewildered. When I awoke I knew what I had to do. I dragged the body into the bathroom and put it in the tub." Burgos described how he had dismembered the girl's body and wrapped her torso in a tablecloth and the limbs in newspaper.

"What were you thinking all this time?" asked Investigation Director Martin.

"Nothing. I felt nauseated."

"Are you sorry for what you did?"

"Well, if I didn't have such a weak character all this would never have happened to me. I wouldn't have brought disgrace on my family like this. That's what Alcira always reproached me for, my weak character."

Burgos was taken to his apartment where, with a pretty young police department clerk taking the part of his victim, he re-enacted the crime, demonstrating the dismemberment with a wooden knife. Police inspectors couldn't help but notice the cruel smile that was on his lips whilst he was cutting.

At his subsequent trial, the jury had no hesitation in delivering their sentence of guilty. Jorge Eduardo Burgos was sentenced to life imprisonment.

3

REGINALD CHRISTIE:
LOVER OF THE DEAD

On November 30th, 1949, twenty-four-year-old Timothy John Evans walked into the police station at Merthyr Vale, South Wales, and made a startling confession. "I have disposed of my wife," he declared. "I put her down a drain."

The police found it hard to take the words of this backward and virtually illiterate van driver seriously, but they were duty-bound to investigate his claim. A call was thus placed to the police in London, and in due course a visit made to Evans's home. There, at 10 Rillington Place, Notting Hill, the ghastly truth of his confession seemed clear. The bodies of not only his wife but also his baby daughter, Geraldine, were found in an outside washhouse. They had both been strangled.

Evans was promptly charged, and came up for trial at the Old Bailey the following January. By then he had withdrawn his confession but was putting forward a story that seemed so improbable that it was hard for anyone to believe it. Evans accused his downstairs neighbour of being the true culprit. He said that his neighbour had attempted to perform an abortion on his wife and that she had died as a consequence. He claimed that her body had been put into a spare room in the house and that was the last he had seen of her. He further claimed that his neighbour had made arrangements for Geraldine to be taken in by a foster family. Evans said that the discovery of the two bodies in the washhouse at his home was as great a shock to him as it was to anyone else.

It was an implausible tale and, not surprisingly, the jury were not convinced. If any of them did have any doubts they were quickly dispelled when Evans' neighbour himself appeared in the witness box. The thin, balding man gave his testimony in a soft, almost childish voice. He said he knew nothing of any abortion and said that at the time of the murder: "I was in bed a lot of the time with the illness I had, which is enteritis and fibrositis in my back." This account was backed up by a statement from his doctor. Clearly, it seemed, Evans was lying. The jury came up with the only verdict that made sense. Timothy John Evans was hanged on March 9th, 1950.

Three years later, however, and there was reason to reconsider the case. The new face in the dock of the Old Bailey cast considerable doubt on what had gone on before. Here was the man that Evans had accused, and though he was only being charged with the murder of his own wife, he was also being held for the murder of five other women and, by his own admission, for the death of Mrs Evans. His name was John Reginald Halliday Christie.

For a man who was to become one of the most horrific killers in British criminal history Christie had a surprisingly normal upbringing. He was born on April 8th, 1898, in Halifax, West Yorkshire, to a family of seven children. An unremarkable child, he was distinguished only by his frailty and his tendency towards hypochondria. School days were not happy. The other children made fun of him, continually calling him a sissy. These taunts hurt the young Christie very deeply, but it was nothing compared to the teasing he received in early adolescence.

Reginald Christie had the misfortune to be introduced

to sex by an older girl who was not the model of discretion. She was quick to make public fun of him for his poor performance. Thereafter he became the butt of innumerable jokes and earned the nickname that never left him: "Reggie No-Dick." Could this have been the seed that later turned Christie into a killer?

More frequently, however, it is another episode in Christie's childhood that is cited as the key to his later twisted development. This was the death of his grandfather. Reggie was just eight years old when it happened, and he was taken to view the body. He was astounded how a man so vital and energetic could now be reduced to this husk. It sparked in the boy a lifelong obsession with the dead. For years afterwards he would visit the local cemetery to peer through cracks in the vaults at the stacked coffins within. It gave the young Christie a peculiar thrill.

Christie quit school when he was fifteen and took a job as a clerk for the Halifax Borough Police. But it didn't last long. He was soon fired on suspicion of theft. He then found work as a projectionist at the Gem Cinema in Halifax.

He was called up for service in 1915 and served in the trenches in France until he was injured by an exploding mustard-gas shell. This caused him to go blind for several months and also rendered him mute for a while. These symptoms were attributed to hysteria rather than physical damage, but they nevertheless allowed Christie to be invalided out of the Army and spend the rest of the war in relative peace. It was during this period of tranquillity that he met Ethel Waddington, the woman who was to become his wife.

Ethel and Reggie married in 1920. It was not a great success. Sexually he fared no better as a married man than he had as a bachelor. Christie later claimed that he was unable to have intercourse for the first two years of marriage, and though this problem was eventually resolved, the couple were never to have children.

Christie also seemed incapable of staying out of trouble. In 1921 he was jailed for theft, and two years later he was in court again, charged with false pretence. By 1923 Ethel had had enough and the couple separated. Ethel stayed with her relatives in Sheffield, Christie moved to London.

In September 1924 Christie was facing another prison sentence for theft. This time, however, the punishment had some effect, for when he was released he seemed to have turned over a new leaf. He got a job as a clerk with a transport company and held it down for five whole years. Alas, by 1929, his basic criminal character had surfaced once more and he was back in court yet again.

This time he was accused of hitting a prostitute over the head with a cricket bat. Christie said it was a "practice shot", but the magistrate called it a murderous attack and jailed him for six months. Four years later he was charged with stealing a car from a priest, and jailed again.

It was whilst he was serving out this last term that Christie wrote to his wife and begged her to visit him. For reasons that no one can adequately explain, she consented to do so, and they somehow managed a reconciliation. On Christie's release in 1933 the couple began to live together again, the decade of separation apparently forgotten. Over the next five years they lodged at various addresses in West London. Then, in 1938, they moved to 10 Rillington Place. The couple occupied three rooms on the ground floor, with exclusive use of the garden.

In 1939 Christie joined the War Reserve Police. He relished wearing his uniform and quickly gained a reputation as an over-officious and tyrannical constable. He also began picking up women and taking them to his home. As later events would show, these women rarely left the house alive.

Ruth Fuerst, a 21-year-old Austrian, was Christie's first

known victim. In his dark blue uniform and peaked cap, the 45-year-old Christie invited her back to 10 Rillington Place some time in late 1943. Conveniently, his wife was away visiting relatives in Sheffield at the time.

When Ruth Fuerst's remains were discovered her body had virtually rotted away, so it is impossible to determine the cause of her death. But we do have Christie's own account of what happened: "One day when this Austrian girl was with me in the flat at Rillington Place, she undressed and wanted me to have intercourse with her," Christie told the police. "I got on to the bed and had intercourse with her. While I was having intercourse with her, I strangled her with a piece of rope. I remember urine and excreta coming away from her. She was completely naked. I tried to put some of her clothes back on her. She had a leopard-skin coat and I wrapped this round her. I took her from the bedroom into the front room and put her under the floorboards. I had to do that because of my wife coming back. I put the remainder of her clothing under the floorboards too...during the [next] afternoon my wife went out. While she was out I pulled the body up from under the floorboards and took it into the outhouse. Later in the day I dug a hole in the garden and in the evening when it was dark, about ten o'clock I should say, I put the body down in the hole and covered it up quickly with earth."

It was approximately a year later that Christie's next victim met her fate. She was a small, plump woman by the name of Muriel Eady. Muriel and her boyfriend had visited the Christies at Rillington Place a number of times before, but one day she arrived alone. Muriel complained of catarrh, and Christie offered her a restorative inhalation.

Christie's readiness to help indicates that he had already developed his ingenious method of gassing victims. It is certainly not beyond the bounds of possibility that he had used it before in crimes we know nothing about.

But, according to the record, Muriel Eady was the first to use the "breathing machine".

Muriel placed her head over a metal tin that had been punched with two holes. Two tubes provided the concoction that she breathed in. Through one came a mixture of Friars Balsam, herbs and other inhalants. These provided some relief from her congestion. They also, however, served another purpose. These heady vapours disguised the smell of what was coming from the other tube. That second tube was connected directly to the gas tap.

"She inhaled the stuff from the tube," Christie later confessed. "I believe I had intercourse with her at the time I strangled her. That night I buried her in the garden."

Christie was always vague about what he did with his victims' corpses. But it is not hard to guess what went on in his deranged mind. With his victims comatose or dead, "Reggie No-Dick" was transformed into a virile, powerful he-man. Copulation with the corpses might have been brief, but at least he did not have any complaints about his performance. He was, in his own mind, a magnificent stud.

Perhaps the real nature of Christie is revealed in what he told the police about the murder of Muriel Eady. Relating how he had carried the unconscious woman to his bedroom, dumped her on the bed and removed her knickers before beginning intercourse and strangling her, he described his feelings as he looked down on her lifeless body: "Once again I experienced that quiet, peaceful thrill. I had no regrets."

Christie's assaults were heavily ritualised. He would ply his victims with drink, then, when they were drunk, he would sit them in a chair with its back to the window and gas them with his "breathing machine". When they were unconscious he would rape them. To heighten his sensation of control, he would take out a rope, his "strangling cord", as he called it, which he kept in the kitchen, and loop it round the victim's neck, tightening it to ensure death. He would also masturbate over their corpses.

With his necrophiliac fantasies fulfilled, Christie would then collect a sample of pubic hair from the victim as a sort of trophy, strip the body and pin a crude nappy on it. Then he would conceal the corpse, usually under the floorboards.

Christie followed this method in all his killings, including the murder of Beryl Evans. This particular death, however, is still shrouded in some mystery. During the course of his trial Christie gave different versions of what happened. In one he describes how he made the pretence of aborting her, before gassing and strangling her. In another he weaves a curious tale of Mrs Evans, despondent over her husband's sexual escapades, asking him to help her die and offering him sex as a reward. His confusing statements about her death are impossible to understand. The one thing of which we can be sure is that it was Christie and not the hapless Tim Evans who was guilty of her murder.

By 1952 Rillington Place had become a slum area. Most of the houses had been converted into flats and bedsits. In the Christies' building, four Jamaican families had moved into flats on the first and second floors. They were noisy, troublesome neighbours and Ethel Christie was particularly upset by their behaviour. She became increasingly nervous and fretful, and her health began to suffer. It was thus, according to Christie, that she came to be his next victim. As he put it : "I was awakened by my wife. She appeared to be convulsive. Her face was blue and she appeared to be choking... I did what I could to restore her breathing but it was hopeless... I couldn't bear to see her , so I got a stocking and tied it around her neck to put her to sleep. I placed her under the floorboards. I thought that was the best way to lay her to rest."

Everybody has their limits, however, and Christie had just found his. Following this "mercy-killing", he began to fall apart. "I was in a state and didn't know what to do", he said. He sold most of his furniture shortly afterwards, keeping only a mattress and blankets, a table and chairs and some crockery and cutlery. For ten weeks, in the bitter cold of winter, he lived in the back room with only his mongrel dog and a cat for company. Were it not for his appetite for murder he might have stayed in that room indefinitely. But the desire to kill eventually got the better of him and he ventured out once more.

Christie murdered three prostitutes in the month that followed. They were twenty-six-year-old Kathleen Maloney and Rita Nelson, who was twenty-five, and six months pregnant. They were killed towards the end of January. Then, on March 6th, he lured his last victim back to Rillington Place: Hectorina MacLennan.

All three corpses were stuffed into a wall cupboard in his kitchen, which he wallpapered over to conceal it and make it seem continuous with the wall. MacLennan was naked except for a brassière and suspender belt. The other two were partly clothed and wrapped in blankets. All three had a cloth between their legs, tied somewhat like a nappy. All had been subjected to sexual intercourse around the time of death.

Christie was now certain that his house reeked of the smell of death. Every day he poured disinfectant down the drains and around the house, hoping to disguise the smell of the decomposing bodies. However, there was very little smell around. The atmospheric conditions in the kitchen caused dehydration. The bodies were in effect mummified. But by now all sense of reality had left the demented killer.

After the last killing, Christie went to pieces entirely. And not without good reason. He now owed rent but he had nothing left to sell. His wife lay rotting under the floorboards and three dead prostitutes occupied the alcove in the kitchen. Two more victims were buried in the garden.

He was desperate to leave the flat, and on Friday, March 13th he managed to arrange just that. He illegally sub-let his three rooms to a couple, taking three months rent in advance. He then took his dog to a vet to be destroyed. On March 20th, 1953, carrying his few possessions in a cheap suitcase, Christie walked out of 10 Rillington Place for the very last time.

The new tenants enjoyed an occupancy of their new flat for just one day before the landlord arrived and unceremoniously evicted them. Then, without further ado, he installed a new tenant of his own choosing, a Mr Beresford Brown.

It was the unfortunate Mr Brown who uncovered Christie's secret. Wanting to put up a bracket on the wall to hold a radio, he discovered the hollow spot. Pulling away a small piece of wallpaper, he found the cupboard behind it. A corner of its door was missing, and Brown shone a torch into the dark interior, illuminating Reginald Christie's gruesome harem.

The police were quickly summoned and Christie's rooms were meticulously searched. The cupboard was opened up, and each body was removed, photographed and examined. All three had been gassed and strangled and all stood in their peculiar nappies.

Underneath the floorboards in the front room police found Ethel Christie's decomposing body, wrapped in a blanket. Although fully dressed, she too had on a nappy. She had been dead for at least three months. Police also found a tobacco tin containing four sets of neatly arranged pubic hair. None had come from the three bodies in the alcove, but one set was believed to have been taken from Ethel. The others must have come from other women, perhaps earlier victims that have never been found.

Digging the garden, the police found human bones. A

femur was actually propping up the garden fence.

The next day the newspapers went wild with headlines about the "House of Horror" and a massive police hunt for Christie was launched. Huge resources were devoted to his capture but, extraordinarily, he was not found for almost a week.

Reginald Christie was finally spotted leaning on the embankment wall near Putney Bridge, gazing wistfully across the Thames. He was taken first to Putney and then to Notting Hill Police stations, where he made a series of statements. Initially he admitted only the "mercy killing" of his wife. Later he confessed to the murders of the three prostitutes. But he refused to say anything about his sexual behaviour or his methods of killing.

At his trial, which began on Monday, June 22nd, 1953, in the No 1 Court at the Old Bailey, Christie was charged only with the murder of his wife, although evidence relating to the other murders was allowed.

In the light of the huge amount of evidence against him it was inconceivable that he would not be found guilty. But Christie hoped to avoid the hangman's noose with a plea of insanity. In his opening speech for the defence Derek Curtis-Bennett QC said: "He is as mad as a March Hare when he kills people. He must be, in my submission, a maniac and a madman ..."

Few could disagree with the counsel's statement. But madness in fact and madness in law are two different things. The jury found Christie guilty and his plea of insanity was rejected. He was sentenced to death.

On the morning of July 15th, 1953, John Reginald Halliday Christie was hanged at Pentonville Prison.

4

DENNIS NILSEN:
THE COMFORT OF CORPSES

Dennis Nilsen was a loner who craved company. The best time in his life were the ten years he spent in the Army. He joined in August 1961, when he was just 15, and revelled in the uniform and in the camaraderie of his peers. He trained as a chef and learnt the skills of butchery before being dispatched to serve in Aden, the Persian Gulf, Cyprus and Germany.

Nilsen enjoyed being surrounded by a whole troupe of mates who knew him by name and would exchange pleasantries with him. He still avoided making any close relationships but it was during this time that he first discovered his homosexuality and, one must assume, enjoyed at least some passing romantic liaisons. One of these liaisons may have been with a youthful private whom Nilsen befriended when he was posted to the Shetland Islands in 1971. Corporal Nilsen made many films of this young man, whom he instructed to lie still and "play dead". This was perhaps the first manifestation of Nilsen's necrophiliac streak.

Nilsen left the Army in 1972 with a fine reference of "exemplary" conduct. He now exchanged the life of a soldier for that of a policeman and was posted as a probationer to Willesden Green station in London. It didn't take him long, however, to realize that the camaraderie of the Force was nothing like that of the Army. He was soon itching to leave.

But at least the job had its advantages. During the course of his duties Constable Nilsen came face to face with London's gay scene and was able to meet many fellow homosexuals. He visited many of the city's gay clubs and pubs. Now, perhaps for the first time, he gave vent to his homosexual passions, and he did so with a vengeance. He had an affair with one man, and smuggled another into his police section room for anal sex.

Nilsen left the Force in November 1973 and, for a while worked as a security guard. That, however, suited him no better. He quit that job too. Finally he resolved it was better to have no job at all and he signed on the dole. But he wasn't unemployed for long. He was persuaded to apply for a clerical post with the Department of Employment, and in due course, he found himself working at the Denmark Street Job Centre in central London.

To his colleagues at this time Nilsen appeared a hostile and prickly character. He made no friends at work and remained reclusive. Away from the Job Centre, however, things were different. Nilsen picked up many young men in the pubs around Soho and would frequently take them back to his home. In those early years he had many affairs, though none seems to have been more significant than another.

In November 1975, however, he made friends with a young man named David Gallichan. Ten years Nilsen's junior, Gallichan was not a homosexual. But he and Nilsen got on well enough and very soon the two men were sharing a flat. Gallichan provided Nilsen with the sense of stability and security that had previously been missing from his life. What Nilsen provided Gallichan with was harder to discern. But they lived together happily enough.

When, in May 1977, Gallichan announced that he could not stand London any more and had taken a job in the country, Nilsen was devastated. He felt rejected and betrayed. He felt no better when Gallichan's place was taken over by a young male prostitute. The relationship didn't work and the boy soon left.

Nilsen's flat at 195 Melrose Avenue, Cricklewood, now felt very empty and friendless. He began to indulge in his morbid fantasies. He started using make-up to give himself the appearance of a corpse, with dark eyes and dead white flesh, and would masturbate whilst looking at this macabre reflection in the mirror. He also began drinking himself into a stupor every night, listening to pop music over headphones with a manic intensity.

Christmas 1978 was a lonely time. Nilsen was all alone in his flat, with only his dog Bleep for company. He was deeply depressed and utterly morose. It was a few days later that he committed his first murder.

Nilsen picked up his victim in a pub in Soho on December 30th. He was a young Irish labourer, a boy still in his teens. Nilsen took him back to his flat that evening and the two slept together. Nilsen would later say that he did not know what happened during the night but when he woke up he found his companion beside him, strangled with a tie. Nilsen washed the corpse in the bath, put it back in bed and attempted to have sex with it. Later, before putting the body under the floorboards, he masturbated over it.

For Nilsen this was a moment of truth. "I took possession of a new kind of flat-mate," he would later declare. He added that he was determined to have company, "even if it was only a body".

Despite his sense of exhilaration, that first killing shocked Nilsen. He was certain he would be found out. He expected the police would be knocking on his door at any moment. and when they didn't he contemplated giving himself up. The only reason he didn't, he later said, was because there would be nobody to take care of his dog.

As the days passed, however, Nilsen's confidence returned. Before long everything was back to normal. He kept the Irishman's body under his floorboards for more than seven months. Then in August he took the body out and burned it on a bonfire in his garden. He burned some rubber tyres as well in an effort to disguise the smell.

On October 31st, 1979, Nilsen enticed his second victim to his flat. He had picked up a young Chinese cook, Andrew Ho, at a pub near Trafalgar Square and the two went back to Melrose Avenue for more drinks. There Nilsen tried to strangle the boy, but Ho managed to fight him off, knocking him unconscious with a brass candlestick. Mr Ho later reported the incident to the police and as a consequence Nilsen found himself being questioned by his ex-colleagues. But he denied all knowledge of the attack, claiming that they had both been drunk and Ho had actually attacked him. The police didn't take it further.

The next murder victim was a 23-year-old Canadian tourist, Kenneth Ockenden. Nilsen had met him in the Princess Louise pub in High Holborn and the two got chatting. Ockenden was not a homosexual but he was happy to have the company of this polite Englishman. The two went back to Nilsen's flat and ate a meal of ham, eggs and chips. Then they bought some drink and settled down for the night. Ockenden listened to music through Nilsen's headphones. It was with the headphone cord that Nilsen strangled him.

Nilsen said later: " I kept him with me for the rest of the night. There was no sex, just caressing etc." He sat the body in an armchair and made up the face with cosmetics. Nilsen spent a while watching TV with Ockenden's corpse and also talking to it before he finally hid it under the floorboards.

In the weeks that followed, Nilsen would frequently take Ockenden's body out from its hiding-place. He would wash it and caress it, and also attempt intercourse of a sort. Later he dissected the body, flushing much of it down the toilet.

Nilsen felt a sense of panic over his crime, especially when he saw a report about the man's disappearance on the television news. But it wasn't as bad as the last time and henceforth, with two murders behind him, he was, he said, able to feel "less emotional" about it. Nilsen had accepted the fact that he was a compulsive killer.

After the Ockenden killing the murder toll climbed rapidly. In May 1980 Nilsen picked up Martyn Duffey, a sixteen-year-old Liverpudlian. He took him to Melrose Avenue where he strangled him and then drowned him in the bath. Next came Billy Sutherland, a 26-year-old Scottish skinhead. Then there was the young man Nilsen called "Mex" because of his Latino appearance. He was followed by an Irish labourer Nilsen picked up in a local pub. Victim number seven was a pathetic young down-and-out who reminded Nilsen of a concentration camp inmate. Nilsen took him home and fed him a sumptuous meal. Then, when the lad was asleep, Nilsen took out a tie and strangled him.

All the killings followed much the same pattern. Nilsen would strangle his victims and then wash them. Later he would lay their corpses out on his bed and masturbate over them. Subsequently he would place them under the floorboards, to take them out again periodically to cuddle, caress or simply to talk to.

To cover the smell of putrefaction, Nilsen invested in a good number of air-fresheners and generous quantities of disinfectant. When eventually the smell became so strong that it could no longer be masked Nilsen retrieved the bodies and dissected them on the kitchen floor. The heads went into plastic bags and the more bulky parts were put into suitcases which he stored in the garden shed. A man once found a plastic bag full of entrails dumped in the street outside. He reported his find to the police but they dismissed it as being simply refuse.

Even with some of the bodies in the shed and their entrails disposed of, however, the corpses were beginning to be a nuisance. Nilsen would not always return them to their proper place under the floorboards and would occasionally forget where he had left them. In September 1980 Nilsen went to get a shirt from the wardrobe and a body fell out on him. Even for him that was a bit of a shock. At that moment he resolved that something had to be done.

It was then that he had the second bonfire in the garden, again adding car tyres to disguise the stench of burning flesh. The fire burned through the day and well into the night. The following morning he used a roller to crush the remaining evidence, the skulls and the bones, into small fragments.

Now the bodies were gone but Nilsen's killing habit lingered and it wasn't long before corpses were building up again.

On November 10th, 1980, he picked up a twenty-six-year-old Scot whom he took home and plied with drink. This Scotsman, however, had a more robust constitution than Nilsen had imagined and fought him off when the ligature went round his neck. He reported the attack to the police but the officers responding to his call concluded that it had just been a homosexual lovers' quarrel and nothing more was done.

A young hippy with long fair hair was Nilsen's next victim, and this time the "quarrel" culminated in the usual killing. A short while afterwards another unnamed Scottish victim was strangled, and joined the corpse of the hippy beneath the floorboards. Victim number ten was Irish. Nilsen said he couldn't remember this killing, alleging that he had woken up with the man dead on his floor. Number 11 was a Cockney skinhead with a dotted line tattooed around his neck with the inscription: "Cut along the dotted line." Nilsen happily obliged.

Nilsen's next victim was a retarded young man aged 24. Malcolm Barlow was an epileptic whom Nilsen found slumped against a wall near his home on September

17th. He had evidently suffered a fit, and Nilsen was charitable enough to order an ambulance to take him into hospital. Barlow was discharged the next day and went back to Melrose Avenue to thank his kind protector. Nilsen later admitted he strangled Barlow simply because he was a "nuisance". Barlow's body was hidden under the sink, later to be placed on another giant bonfire.

At the end of the summer of 1981 Nilsen's landlord told him he was thinking of developing the building in Melrose Avenue and asked Nilsen if he would be willing to leave. He offered his tenant a £1,000 sweetener. Nilsen readily accepted. It was too good to refuse. The only problem was the bodies that littered his flat. The bonfire was already on Nilsen's mind as he was strangling the unfortunate Barlow.

On the evening of October 4th, 1981, everything was in order. The flat at Melrose Avenue was clear of bodies and Nilsen's suitcases and boxes were piled up and packed. The following day he would move to Muswell Hill. Here, with his dog Bleep, he would occupy a small flat at the very top of a house at 23 Cranley Gardens. It consisted of only two rooms plus a kitchen and a bathroom, but for a single man, it was more than adequate. For Nilsen, however, there was one obvious drawback. There was no back garden. From now on there could be no more fires. Future victims would have to disappear by other means.

The first victim to be killed at Cranley Gardens was known to Nilsen only as "John the Guardsman". He was later identified as John Howlett, a 23-year-old drifter from High Wycombe in Buckinghamshire. The two had met in a pub and Nilsen had invited Howlett back to his home for a drink. When his guest seemed to make himself too comfortable Nilsen got annoyed. "I didn't know you were moving in," he remarked acidly. When the man fell into a drunken stupor Nilsen was quick to get his revenge. He put a ligature round his neck. "I think it's time you went," he snapped. He throttled Howlett into unconsciousness and then placed him in the bath to drown.

Nilsen dissected his victim with speed. He boiled the head in a large pot and flushed the internal organs and some flesh down the toilet. The rest he packed into a tea-chest which stood in the corner of the flat. The larger bones he put out in the dustbin for collection.

The following month, April 1982, Nilsen met Carl Stotter, a twenty-one-year-old drag artiste who was known professionally as "Blondie". He took him back to Cranley Gardens and they went to bed together.

In the middle of the night Stotter woke up in a sweat. He had dreamt he was being strangled and had been too weak to resist. He was being lifted and carried, then plunged into a bath full of water. His head was pushed down several times. Finally he lost consciousness.

Stotter woke up in bed, with Nilsen's dog licking his face. In fact Nilsen had thought he had succeeded in killing him and was very surprised when the man started moving. But he was quick to adapt to the situation. Nilsen made every attempt to help Stotter recover, turning on all the bars of the electric fire to warm him. Nilsen tried to persuade Stotter that he must have got his neck stuck in the zipper of the sleeping bag and choked himself. Stotter almost believed him, but made a hasty departure all the same.

Nilsen's next killing occurred some time in mid-1982. Graham Allan was a 28-year-old drug addict whom Nilsen strangled and then dissected in the bath. Then, on New Year's Day, another potential candidate had a lucky escape. Nilsen attempted to strangle Toshimitu Ozawa, a young Japanese student. But Ozawa managed to fight him off and fled the house.

Stephen Sinclair was not so lucky. He was killed on the night of January 26th, 1983. The following morning Nilsen lay beside the dead body with an erection.

Nilsen later told the police of how he attempted to

dispose of Sinclair. "I put the head in a pot, popped the lid on and lit the stove. When the head was coming to the boil I turned the pot down to simmer, then I took the dog out for a walk. Later I watched TV as the head was simmering." Most of Sinclair's dissected corpse was later found in two black refuse bags in the wardrobe. Nilsen had tried to flush pieces of flesh down the toilet, but the drains were blocked.

A few days later the residents of the other flats in the building found their toilets were also blocked, and they phoned the landlord to complain. He arranged for a plumber to call on Saturday, February 5th. The plumber, however, quickly decided that the job was too big for him and suggested that the landlord contact DynoRod. This he duly did.

The DynoRod engineer arrived at 6.15 p.m. on Tuesday. He lifted the manhole cover and climbed down into the sewer. There was a revolting smell, and in the light of his torch he noted what looked like lumps of meat blocking the outlet pipes. He could see it would be a difficult job, and arranged to come back the following day. Before leaving, however, he phoned his boss and reported the grim find.

That night Nilsen went down into the sewer and removed most of the flesh, putting it into plastic carrier bags and throwing these over the back garden hedge. But his neighbours had seen him at his midnight task.

Nilsen knew his luck was running out. The next day would be crucial. He thought of suicide, but couldn't bear the notion of leaving his dog Bleep. So instead he went to work as usual. That night, before leaving, he left a note on his desk. It said that if he were to be arrested there would be no truth in reports that he had killed himself in his cell.

When Nilsen returned home on the evening of February 9th he found the police waiting for him. "I've come about your drains," said Detective Chief Inspector Peter Jay.

"Why should the police be interested in drains?" replied Nilsen.

"The reason I am interested in your drains is that they are blocked with human remains."

"Good God!" cried Nilsen. "That's terrible. Where did they come from?"

"Don't mess about," said the Chief Inspector. "Where's the rest of the body?"

Nilsen confessed immediately. "It's a relief to get it off my mind," he said.

The questioning of Nilsen began on February 11th at Hornsey Police Station. Detectives listened in horror as Nilsen, with dispassionate calm, dictated a precise and detailed account of his many murders. He said he was happy that he had been caught now because "if I had been arrested at sixty-five years of age there might have been thousands of bodies behind me".

The trial of Nilsen began at the Old Bailey on Monday October 24th, 1983. During the course of the proceedings the jury learnt of Nilsen's early background, his unhappy childhood in Scotland, the early divorce of his parents and the death of his grandfather. Nilsen had seen the man's corpse and it had apparently had a profound effect on him. He was just seven years old at the time. They also heard of his career in the Army and, later in the Civil Service. His defence tried to argue that his problem dated back to a personality disorder of his childhood. He was suffering, they said, from a "False Self Syndrome."

But could this explain or excuse all the murders? The jury thought not. After 24 hours of debate they finally returned a majority verdict of guilty on all six counts of murder with which Nilsen was charged. On Friday, November 4th, 1983 he was sentenced to life imprisonment.

5

HEIDNIK'S HOUSE OF HORROR

Josefina Rivera was black, 26 years old and the mother of three infant children. She was also a prostitute. She lived with her boyfriend, Vincent Nelson, in a third-floor apartment on North Sixth Street, Philadelphia.

At around 5.30 p.m. on November 20th, 1987, Josefina told Vincent that she was going shopping. But Josefina didn't go shopping. Instead she went to the corner of Third Street and Girard Avenue and spent the evening plying for custom.

At around 11 o'clock Josefina's head turned when a shiny Cadillac drove up to the kerb. The driver, a man somewhat older than her, was white, wore glasses and had a reddish-brown beard. He was tall and square-shouldered. His clothes were casual but smart.

Josefina thought he seemed nice enough, for a client, and when they had agreed on a price she got into his car and they drove to his house at 3520 North Marshall Street.

It was after sex that the man showed his true brutality. He grabbed Josefina around the neck and began to throttle her. The girl passed out, and the next thing she knew she was being dragged into the basement where she was shackled to a sewer pipe. She watched as her captor dug a pit in the concrete floor, fearing it was going to be her grave. But he assured her that the hole was only for punishment if she misbehaved. He told her he was attracted to black women and planned to have ten captive in the cellar and have children by them all. "We'll be one happy family."

Forty-four-year-old Gary Heidnik, the owner of 3520 North Marshall Street, was a bizarre individual. Invalided out of the Army in 1963, he suffered from persistent psychiatric problems and had been admitted to mental hospitals no fewer than 21 times. His sexual appetite was both enormous and unusual. He only enjoyed sleeping with black women, usually two or three at a time. His Filipino wife, Betty Disto, left him after only a few weeks of marriage when she came home to find him in bed with three others. Heidnik tried to assure her that this was a normal custom for American males but Betty was unconvinced. After being subjected to anal rape by her husband, she walked out.

But Heidnik had his good side. Mindy Lawrence, a long-term girlfriend, liked him a lot. "He had a nice smile and he made you laugh," she said. He was also an astute businessman. In 1971 he established the United Church of Ministers of God, ordained himself as a bishop and, playing the stock market under the cover of this "church", made himself a substantial fortune.

It was this fortune that bought him the house and the Cadillac which had so impressed the unfortunate Josefina.

Josefina Rivera was repeatedly raped by Heidnik during her first day of capture. She was also forced to perform oral sex on him. She did try to escape once. She managed to force open a window and scream for help. Nobody came, but Heidnik heard her, beat her, then threw her in the pit. After that Josefina was left alone, with a radio playing rock music at full volume to drown out any more cries for help.

Three days later Heidnik brought his second prisoner into the basement. She was 24-year-old Sandra Lindsay. He told Josefina and Sandra that the world was full of "impure" people. He wanted Josefina and Sandra to bear his children and help him begin a "purified" family.

One by one, Heidnik brought more women home. On December 22nd, 19-year-old Gail Midley accepted Heidnik's invitation to dinner and then went home with him. "I went in the living-room," she said. "He brought me a beer. But then he got up and grabbed my neck and shook me half to death. Then he took me down the cellar."

On January 1st, 1987, they were joined by yet another, Deborah Dudley, a forceful and quick-tempered 23-year-old. Four weeks later Tammy Kramer, 18, disappeared from her family home. She too ended up in Heidnik's cellar. Then on March 20th Heidnik picked up another prostitute, 24-year-old Patty Conrad.

All these unfortunate women were kept in the cellar. They were stripped and chained and continuously forced to satisfy Heidnik's brutal cravings. They also had to put up with his sadistic psychological games, which he hoped would guarantee their obedience.

He played one girl off against the other to see who would obey his commands and who wouldn't, who would "rat" on the others and who wouldn't. He turned on the music and pretended to leave the house. Then he listened to see if any of them screamed for help. If they did he turned up the volume of the music and tortured them. He'd gag them to stifle their screams and then stick screwdrivers into their ears until blood spurted out. That way, if they screamed for help, they wouldn't be able to hear if anyone responded. Sometimes, he hooked live wires to their metal shackles.

One day in early February Sandra Lindsay misbehaved. For punishment, Heidnik chained her arms to a beam and let her hang for eight hours. She started vomiting, then she lost consciousness. When Heidnik unchained her she fell and hit her head on the floor. He carried her body upstairs, but none of the other captives knew if she was dead or alive.

For the next few hours a power saw buzzed over the music and a horrible smell filled the house. The stench lingered for three or four days, and whenever Heidnik came down to have sex with the women the rotten smell came with him. It was later deduced to be the smell of Sandra's boiling flesh. In the days that followed Heidnik would serve her flesh to his other captors, mixing it in with the dog food that was their diet so they did not realise what they were eating.

In March, Debbie Dudley refused to co-operate with Heidnik any longer. For her punishment she went into the pit. He filled it with water and attached electrical wires to her chains. Then he plugged the cord into an outlet and electrocuted her. Heidnik stored Debbie's body in a freezer in the basement and later dumped it in some woods in New Jersey.

As time went on, Josefina gained Heidnik's confidence. Occasionally, he allowed her freedom from her bondage, but she had always been too terrified to try to escape. "I feared for my safety and the safety of the other girls," she told detectives. "Gary said he'd kill me if I left, or if I didn't help him." But she was still looking out for a chance for freedom and, on March 27th, that chance arrived.

Josefina told Heidnik that she'd help him find a new girl to replace Debbie Dudley. For hours they cruised the streets to find the new recruit. When they arrived at a minimart, Josefina told him to stop the car and let her out. This was where she'd find the new girl for him. Heidnik hesitated. He almost drove away. But finally he agreed, warning Josefina again that he'd kill her if she tried anything funny.

Josefina got out of the car. Heidnik waited inside. As soon as she was out of his sight Josefina broke into a desperate run. She dashed to her boyfriend's apartment and banged on the door frantically. She told him the whole extraordinary story. He could hardly believe it, but together, they called the police.

By 4 a.m. search warrants were approved, and minutes later, three detectives broke down the front door of Gary Heidnik's home.

It was ominously quiet. The only sounds were their footsteps, creaking on the rickety wooden stairway as they slowly descended towards the torture chamber. There were no cries for help as their flashlight beams pierced the pitch blackness below, and they began to doubt Josefina Rivera's wild story. But their disbelief was short-lived.

They saw Gail Midley first. Then Tammy Kramer. Both were chained to the sewer pipes with muffler clamps and handcuffs. Patty Conrad was found inside the pit.

"When we heard the banging," Gail Midley later explained, "we kept quiet because he usually tested us to see if we were going to scream or holler, so he could beat the shit out of us. When we seen the flashlights and all the cops and stuff coming, and they said, 'Everything is all right, y'all free now,' then we knew we were safe."

All three women appeared to be dehydrated and malnourished. It was later learned that all they had been given to eat was bread, water, dog food and dog biscuits. Soon an ambulance was rushing the three women to hospital.

Police officers now began a search of the house. They started in the kitchen, and within minutes, realised that Josefina had not been exaggerating.

Two handless forearms, one upper arm and pieces of thigh were found in the freezer, wrapped in plastic bags. Smaller chunks of cooked body parts and charred bone fragments were found in the oven.

All day long bulldozers ploughed up the front yard and the rear area of the house was excavated in a search for human remains. Forensic technicians sifted through every bit of dirt and grime. Detectives went through all Heidnik's papers to find some evidence.

Before long rumours about what had gone on in the house of horror had leaked out. A crowd of spectators gathered around 3520 North Marshall Street, everyone straining to catch sight of what was going on.

"That ain't no dog bone," a voice in the crowd announced when an investigator dropped a large object into a plastic bag. The Philadelphia police department kept silent.

Gary Heidnik's trial began on June 20th, 1988 and it was obvious from the outset that his defence tactic would be to claim insanity. His council didn't even bother to argue the question of guilt.

"My client is not innocent," declared Charles Peruto, "He is very guilty. This is not a case of whodunit. This is a case of why it was done. He is relying on a defence of mental infirmity. His criminal acts will show him to be insane."

In his closing speech for the defence, Peruto told the jury: "What was Gary Heidnik's purpose? His purpose was to raise ten kids, not to kill anybody." He said of Heidnik's captives that one was retarded and three were prostitutes.

"As sick as it is," he went on, "these were his chosen people. These were the girls he wanted to reproduce with. Is that sane?"

District Attorney Gallagher was not confounded. "Just because someone does bizarre acts, the law doesn't recognise them as insane... What he did was premeditated, deliberate murder."

On July 1st, 1989, the jury found Gary Heidnik guilty on all counts. He was sentenced to two death sentences.

Heidnik currently lives on Pennsylvania's Death Row isolated from all the other prisoners. He eats alone, showers alone and is watched at all times. He is likely to remain there for some time.

6

PETER KÜRTEN:
THE MONSTER OF DÜSSELDORF

Many people associate sex with love, others associate it with pleasure. For Peter Kürten, however, sex was always linked with pain, death and blood.

Where this association began is anyone's guess, but one can safely assume that it started early in his life. Peter Kürten was born on May 26th, 1883 and was brought up in a house that was charged with an atmosphere of deviant sex. One of a family of thirteen, Peter's father was a violent drunk who often forced his wife to have intercourse in the children's bedroom. As they all slept together, the young Kürten also witnessed the sexual awakening of his sisters. Whether he ever had intercourse with his siblings is open to doubt, but he certainly witnessed his father's attentions to them; Herr Kürten was subsequently sentenced to three years' imprisonment for incest. Peter was also a witness and a participator in even more deviant practice. The local dog-catcher lived in their house and instructed the boy in methods of torturing animals, and also taught him how to masturbate them. By the time he was just eight, Peter Kürten had proved himself to be the dog-catcher's most accomplished student.

According to his later confession, Kürten committed his first murder when he was nine years old. While playing on a raft on the river Rhine he pushed a playmate over the side and held his head underwater. A friend jumped in to try and rescue the boy, but Kürten pushed him under the raft and he died too.

Perhaps the most significant moment in Peter Kürten's young life came just before his thirteenth birthday. It was then that he began practising bestiality. As he would later recall, his first climax came in the company of a sheep. He ejaculated during intercourse at the very same time as he stabbed the poor animal in the throat. From this moment on the link between sex and blood never left Kürten's mind. Pigs and goats became his subsequent victims.

Peter Kürten left home when he was sixteen and made his way to Coblenz. There he lived with a prostitute whose masochistic inclinations increased Kürten's tendencies to sadism. She also reinforced his association of sex with pain. Their relationship didn't last long, however, because within a year Kürten was arrested for petty theft and sent to prison for the first time. It was a two-year sentence, but in the event only the first sentence of a total of seventeen that he would eventually serve, taking up twenty-seven years of his life. With each new jail sentence for burglary or assault his sado-sexual compulsions were reinforced and his desire to lash out at society grew. Kürten deliberately violated prison rules so that he could be put in solitary confinement, where he passed his time daydreaming about new tortures to inflict on the world.

When he was released in 1899 he lived with another prostitute. She was twice his age but, like his first partner, a woman inclined to masochism. According to Kürten's later police confession, it was during this year that he committed his first adult murder. He said he strangled a girl while having sex with her in the forest. However, there is no police record of this incident.

In the years that followed, Kürten was in and out of prison with alarming regularity. His crimes included arson and assault, and he was also accused of maltreating a servant girl during intercourse, but mostly he was charged with burglary. Following his release on May 25th, 1953 he broke into the private rooms of the Klein family, owners of a public house in Köln-Mülheim. The family were out at a fair but their young daughter, 13-year-old Christine, lay asleep in her room. Kürten reached for her neck and choked her into unconsciousness before cutting her throat with a knife and then penetrating her sexual organs with his fingers.

That same year Kürten attacked four other victims, though none of them fatally. Two women he attempted to strangle, and a young couple he knocked into unconsciousness with a hatchet. But if this was going to be a career it was cut short by yet another term in imprisonment. In 1913 Kürten was jailed for eight years.

When Kürten was released he met his future wife. Three years his senior, she too had been in prison for shooting her unfaithful lover. Why he was attracted to her is difficult to say, but she was to be his port in a storm. He never ill-treated her, but showed her great respect. She was the only individual for whom Kürten felt any sense of affection. They married in 1923 and she only had the barest insight into his sadistic nature. In the two years following their marriage they lived in Altenberg and life was relatively normal. Kürten was twice charged with sadistic maltreatment of servant girls but the cases never came to court.

In 1925 they moved to Düsseldorf and to their new house at 71 Mettmännerstrasse. Here Kürten's progression was slow but steady. In the first year there were three attempted strangulations of women, the following year, one, and in 1927 five cases of arson and one attempted strangulation. In the first few weeks of 1929 there were six more arson attacks on barns and haystacks. Then on February 3rd, 1929 came the attack on Frau Apollonia Kühn. To most commentators it was with this assault that the Düsseldorf monster's reign of terror began.

Frau Kühn was walking through the streets of the city when a man came up behind her, grabbed her by the tunic and stabbed her twenty-four times with a pair of scissors. Her injuries were horrific but she survived.

A week later, however, the remains of not so lucky a victim were discovered. The body of eight-year old Rosa Ohliger was found near Düsseldorf's Vinzenz church. She had been stabbed thirteen times and the killer had doused her with petrol in an attempt to set her on fire. The girl had injuries to her genitals and her hymen was torn. Ejaculation had not taken place within her vagina but semen was found on her knickers.

This horrific attack, however, had not been enough to sate Kürten's blood lust. Three days later he attacked a drunken 45-year-old mechanic, Rudolf Scheer, who was on his way home on the road to Flingern. Kürten inflicted many stab wounds, and as his victim lay dying he drank the blood that came spilling out of him.

The police were baffled by these attacks. They had not a clue as to what madman might have committed them. But then, on April 29th, a lunatic by the name of Stausberg was arrested for attacking two women. He confessed not only to these assaults but also to the murders. The police thought they had their man, and indeed that was the way it seemed, for the Düsseldorf killings came to an abrupt stop. Then, in August 1929, they began yet again.

On August 11th Maria Hahn was stabbed in the throat and her dead body was buried in the ground. Later Kürten would return to kiss and fondle the corpse. When Maria Hahn's body was eventually discovered there was evidence that suggested Kürten indulged in necrophilia. Both her anus and her vagina had been penetrated, and though no semen was found, soil and leaf fragments were. These had evidently been forced into the corpse during an attempt at intercourse.

A little more than a week later, on August 21st, there was another victim. Frau Mantel was stabbed in the back. Later that same evening Anna Goldhausen and a man called Gustav Kornblum were stabbed in a similar fashion. Miraculously, all three survived.

On August 24th, a double murder stunned the city. The bodies of two girls, 5-year-old Gertrude Hamacher and 15-year-old Louise Lenzen, were found, strangled and stabbed, in an allotment close to their homes. Neither had been sexually assaulted.

Twelve hours later Gertrude Schulte, a 26-year-old domestic servant, was on her way to a local fair. Kürten accompanied her through the woods and then made a pass at her. She refused his sexual advances. "I'd rather die," she said. "Well, die then," said Kürten, stabbing her repeatedly and viciously. So violently did he stab her that the blade broke off in her spine. Frau Schulte survived, though she remained in hospital for a long time. That month there were three more unsuccessful assaults.

By the end of September Kürten had evidently lost confidence in his scissors. On September 24th his next victim, a servant girl named Ida Reuter, was bludgeoned to death with a hammer in fields outside the city. Her body was left with her legs splayed wide apart and her genitals showing. Sperm was found in her vagina.

On October 12th the body of Elizabeth Dorrier was found on the banks of the river Düssel. She had been battered about the head with a hammer and her vagina had been injured. She was still alive, but only barely. She died in hospital the following day without ever regaining consciousness.

Later that month there were two more attacks on the same day on different sides of the city. Thirty-four-year-old housewife Frau Meurer was rendered unconscious and Frau Wanders, a prostitute, was also assaulted. Both survived.

On November 7th, five-year-old Gertrude Albermann went missing. Her body was found two days later, lying in a factory yard beside nettles and brick rubble. She had been strangled and stabbed at least 30 times. Her knickers had been torn, and there were injuries to her vagina and anus.

The city was now in a panic, all the more so when it was revealed that the murderer had written to the newspapers stating that he had killed the child and telling them where her body could be found. The police investigation, which had already been vigorous, now became manic. Ironically, however, the murders had already come to an end. Though in the months that followed a number of assaults would be reported, the Monster of Düsseldorf, the "Vampire," as he was now being called, would kill no more.

It was the attempted strangulation of twenty-one-year-old Maria Budlick on May 14th, 1930, which finally led to Kürten's arrest. Maria had travelled from Cologne to Düsseldorf in the hope of finding work. At the station she was accosted by a man who offered to help her find a bed for the night. He had led her away and into Volksgarten Park. The girl was becoming alarmed and was relieved when a kindly-looking stranger intervened and angrily denounced the man as a pervert.

Kürten, for it was he who had come to the girl's rescue, offered to take her back to his flat and gave her a hot meal. Then he agreed to take her to a hostel. They rode the tram to the edge of the city and then walked together into the Grafenburg Woods. It was in these woods that Maria realised that her new friend was no saviour. Kürten turned to her, gave her a rough kiss and demanded sex. The girl refused, so Kürten grabbed her and ripped off her knickers.

Inexplicably, however, this time Kürten didn't go through with the usual assault. Instead he asked the girl if she could remember where he lived. Wisely she said she did not. Kürten then turned and walked away.

Maria Budlick didn't inform the police or indeed tell anyone about the attack. But she did write a letter to a friend mentioning the incident. What this friend would have done with the news is anyone's guess. But in one of those peculiar turns of fate Budlick mis-addressed the envelope and the letter arrived at the home of a certain Frau Brugmann.

Frau Brugmann took the missive to the police, who then tracked down Frau Budlick. It was a long shot that she had had an encounter with the Düsseldorf Monster but worth a chance.

Maria remembered that it was on Mettmännerstrasse that her attacker lived but she had no idea of the number. Walking down the street with police, however, she recognised the building and led the officers inside.

Kürten saw the detectives in the foyer talking to his landlady and fled out of the back door.

That night Peter Kürten met his wife as she was coming home from the restaurant where she worked. He confessed everything to her. At first she didn't believe him, but then as he gave her more and more details of the crimes, she was convinced he was telling the truth. At first she suggested a suicide pact but Kürten persuaded her to do the sensible thing and turn him in, thus collecting a share of the sizeable reward that was now on offer for the killer's arrest.

On May 24th, 1930, Frau Kürten went to the police station and told them that her husband was the Düsseldorf murderer. That afternoon, outside St. Rochus church, she met her husband in the company of four armed policemen. Kürten smiled reassuringly and told them not to be afraid. He was taken into police custody quite peaceably.

Kürten cooperated fully and immediately made a full confession, although he was later to withdraw it. He was charged in court on June 30th, and was remanded in custody until his trial in April 1931.

It was during this year that the psychiatrist Dr Karl Berg examined him, finally publishing a book, *The Sadist*, which recounted Peter Kürten's extraordinary life and behaviour.

Berg was impressed with Kürten's frankness, intelligence and honesty. For his part Kürten was also impressed with the doctor, and attempted to join in the psychological unravelling with him.

"Every evening when my wife was at work I went prowling about for a victim," said Kürten. "The sex urge was always strong in me, particularly during the last years. But it was increased by the deeds themselves. That was why I had to go out again and again to look for a victim..."

Asked how he managed to have normal sexual relations with his wife, he replied that it had been with great difficulty. He had to fill his head with sadistic fantasies before he could succeed. "The main thing with me was to see blood..."The sound of gushing blood always aroused him, he said, and he illustrated this by recalling a day when he was looking for a victim in the Hofgarten park. "I noticed a swan sleeping at the edge of the lake. I cut its throat. The blood spurted up and I drank from the stump and ejaculated."

Kürten's trial began on April 13th, 1931. He was charged with nine murders and seven attempted murders. His defence was to offer a plea of insanity but it was not accepted.

The jury was out for an hour and a half, returning with guilty verdicts on all charges. He was sentenced to death nine times and refused appeal.

On the morning of July 2nd, 1931, Peter Kürten was guillotined in the courtyard of Klingelputz Prison in Cologne. Seconds before the blade fell Kürten turned to his executioner and asked: "After my head has been chopped off will I still be able to hear the sound of my own blood rushing from the stump of my neck? That, even for just a moment, would be the pleasure to end all pleasures."

7

THE BODY IN THE BAG

Something was lying in the road outside Georgia Walters's house on East Penn Street, Long Beach, New York. It was a yellow bundle of some kind, a bag perhaps, and Georgia thought it strange that someone should have left it in the middle of the traffic. But she didn't go over to investigate. Instead she got into her car and drove off to church. It was just after 9 a.m. on Sunday, February 11th, 1990.

When she returned shortly after 11 o'clock, however, the bag was still there, and now Georgia decided to go and have a look. But, as she neared the object she stopped in her tracks. It was a bag all right, a yellow nylon laundry bag, but it was full of something that didn't look like clothes. Long tresses of blonde hair spilled out of the opening. Dark red splotches stained the synthetic fabric.

Georgia ran to her house and called her husband, a lieutenant with the New York City police department. He came out and walked over to the bundle. One peek inside was all he needed to determine that the city had another homicide on its hands.

The corpse in the bag was that of a small, young blonde woman. She was wearing nothing but a man's white T-shirt. There were bruises and cuts on her face and throat. Her right eye was blackened and her lip was swollen. An autopsy later revealed that she had been strangled and had been dead for several hours. Her fingerprints were taken and the police computer came up with her name. She was Stephanie Krut, from Far Rockaway in Queens. Her prints were on file because she had been arrested several times for prostitution. She was just nineteen years old.

The subsequent police investigation revealed that Stephanie had last been seen around 1 a.m. on that Sunday morning. Witnesses remembered seeing her standing on a street corner, either buying drugs or seeing a client. One woman gave a description of a man she had seen with the prostitute, but he wasn't traced. Another put a name to an alternative suspect, but he had an alibi. Numerous other lines of enquiry were followed, but they all came to a dead end. The months went by and the police had got nowhere.

Then, on the night before Halloween on Tuesday, October 30th, 1990, another body in a bag was discovered. A small, naked black woman, once apparently pretty but now horribly bruised, was found wrapped in a white bedspread inside a navy blue garment bag. Her name was Mayra Eusebio and she was 25 years old. Mayra, like Stephanie Krut, was a prostitute.

This second killing was extremely worrying. The similarities of the cases meant it was almost certain that the same person had been responsible. Police began to fear that a serial killer had emerged. But at least with this second victim there was also a ray of hope. This time the killer had left a clue. Hidden in a fold of the bag was a white identification tag with a name and phone number written on it. The garment bag evidently belonged to one Peter Varese who worked in an Italian restaurant in Brooklyn Heights.

Varese was picked up and interviewed by the police. He was a calm, well-mannered and obliging young man who plainly had no knowledge of the crimes or any interest in them, and it did not take the police long to conclude that he was not the villain they were after. One of Varese's relatives, however, was an altogether different breed. Thirty-seven-year-old Allen J. Gormely Jr. was a deeply suspicious character with a chequered history of work in the seedier clubs of Greenwich Village and Chelsea. He was a known cocaine and heroin user and, as investigators later learned, a man with a predilection for rough sex. Furthermore, he lived in Long Beach, the area where both bodies had been found. Gormely was duly brought in for questioning, and after a prolonged interview asked to take a lie-detector test. He consented to the request but failed the test miserably. He was then warned that DNA testing would be able to prove beyond doubt that he was the villain.

He continued to deny the crime for a while and then concocted some elaborate stories to try and explain how it might appear that he was guilty. Finally, however, he made a confession.

Allen Gormely described how he had met Mayra Eusebio and that she had come to his house at about 7.30 on October 30th. He gave details of their sexual exploits together and their shared drug-taking. He then said that Mayra had asked him for money. He claimed she had suddenly become angry and had tried to attack him.

He grabbed Mayra from behind, he said, and, forcing his right arm under her chin and his left arm around her chest, he squeezed the tiny woman with both arms. Mayra shook and convulsed until finally she went limp in his arms. He laid her on the bed. She didn't move. Foam dribbled out of her mouth. Gormely then knew that she was dead.

Scared by what he had done, Gormely then wrapped the dead woman in a white bedspread and put her in a chair. He went to the closet, found the garment bag he'd taken from Varese's house and zipped Mayra up inside it. Then he took the bundle out to his car, put it on the front seat and drove off. Gormely claimed he spent a while driving through the streets hoping to find an appropriate place to dispose of his gruesome cargo. He finally dropped it off at a dark spot in Long Beach. He then returned home and went to bed.

Gormely presented the murder as if it had been entirely accidental, and he continued to do so even when he was shown a photograph of Stephanie Krut. To begin with he denied ever having seen this first victim. Eventually, however, he admitted this killing too, and he explained it in a similar way.

The killer told another sordid story of sweaty sex and crack cocaine. Once more he claimed he was entirely placid until Stephanie asked for money and became violent. They tussled, she bit him, he punched, then she came at him again. He pushed her hard and she fell backwards, hitting her head against a chair. He hit her several more times before he finally got behind her and, just as with Mayra, forced his arm under her chin. Gormely said that all he wanted to do was stop her screaming. He never meant to kill her.

When he saw she was dead, however, he was quick to deal with the situation. He wiped up Stephanie's blood with a towel and then emptied out the clothes from a yellow laundry bag and stuffed Stephanie's body inside. She was still wearing a T-shirt he'd given her earlier in the day. Just after midnight he lugged the bag out to his car, put it on the front seat and drove off. On East Penn Street he slowed down, opened the car door and gave the bundle a push.

The detectives listened to his story in silence. It was clear that Gormley was not telling the whole truth, but it was all they needed. There was no doubt he was the killer.

On April 30th, 1992, Allen J. Gormely Jr. was convicted on two counts of second-degree murder. He was sentenced to 50 years to life.

8

RATTLESNAKES FOR AN
UNWANTED WIFE

Mary James died on August 5th, 1935. She had apparently stumbled into the fish pond in the garden of her
Los Angeles home and drowned. It could have been an
accident. Mary was known to have fainting fits, and she
was also pregnant. It was therefore possible, reasoned
her doctor, that she had fainted and fallen into the shallow pool. Possible, but not likely. Could any person in a
faint fall into cold water and not be revived by the shock
of it? And even if Mary did, that would not explain the
little puncture marks that were found on her leg and
foot.

Then there was the question of her husband. Robert
James, a barber by trade, had wed Mary a few months
previously, but she wasn't his first wife. James had been
married five times before. There had been three divorces
and one annulment. And there had been one death.
James's fifth wife had drowned in the bath. Two wives
drowned by accident? It was beyond belief.

The police had no doubts that James was the killer.
The problem was they had no evidence to back them up.
Days turned into weeks and weeks into months and still
there was nothing to prove Robert James's guilt. But
then, in May 1936, they finally had the breakthrough
they needed.

Pat Foley, a veteran reporter for the Los Angeles

Herald, had dropped into a saloon near James's home for a swift drink when the barman came over to chat with him. "This might be a story for you," he said.

The barman went on to relate how a customer, an ex-sailor who currently ran a hot-dog stand at the local beach, had been in the bar earlier that day and, much the worse for drink, had confided that he had once helped a man kill his wife. As the barman continued with the story, Foley was left in no doubt as to what it might mean.

Later that day the ex-sailor was in police custody, repeating his story in more sober tones. At first he denied everything but then it all spilled out.

"I was drunk," he mumbled. "This guy offered me a lot of money."

"What was his name?"

"James. Robert James."

The ex-sailor then went on to say how he had been in James' barber shop one day and happened to mention he was having money problems. James told the man to meet him after the shop was closed, saying he might have a job going. They met that same night, and it was then that Robert James had told him of his plan.

James said he wanted to murder his wife and would pay him well for his assistance. "I was shocked at first," said the man. "I turned him down cold. But I needed the dough real bad."

The ex-seaman went on to describe how James had decided to kill his wife using live rattlesnakes and how he wanted to put the plan into action. "He gave me the money to buy two snakes from a reptile farm and so I went and bought two middle-sized ones. But he insisted we try them first to be sure their venom was strong enough to kill. He bought a live rabbit and we put it in the box. Both the snakes struck it. But the rabbit didn't die. It swelled up like a balloon, but it didn't die.

"Then we tried two other snakes and a fresh rabbit.

But that one lived through the bites, too. We even tried Black Widow spiders, and they didn't work either. But at last I located two large rattlesnakes at "Snake Joe" Houtenbrink's snake farm that were guaranteed to be deadly. One was called "Lightning," the other "Lethal". They were five feet long and four inches thick at their middles. James was very pleased."

The ex-sailor had now got into his stride and as the officers looked on in disbelief, he boldly continued with his story. He told how he, James and Mary all got together over some drinks and how James put some pills into Mary's glass. Then, when she was asleep, the two of them grabbed her leg and forced it into the cage where the two snakes were resting. After about five minutes, James pulled her leg out. There were several deep punctures in the flesh, each marked by a droplet of blood and each beginning to have a purple swelling around it.

"That should do it! That should surely do it!" James cried.

But it didn't. The two men carried on drinking. They finished one bottle and started on another but Mary still breathed. At last James could stand it no longer. "Start the water in the bath!" he ordered. "I've got to get this over with." They filled the tub and carried Mrs James to the bathroom. James held her head under water. She wriggled a few times, then her body went limp. The two men then carried her body out to the garden and laid it down with her head under the water in the fishpond. Then they parted ways.

When shown the ex-sailor's testimony James admitted the story was true, and he was immediately charged with the first-degree murder of his wife. Before the trial, however, he retracted his confession, claiming that it had been taken from him under duress. Instead he claimed insanity.

The trial of Robert James during the summer of 1936 lasted five weeks and outranked any spectacular turned out in nearby Hollywood. Newspapers hired top movie writers to play up the bizarre story, to lend it a weird drama it didn't really need. The accomplice who had turned state's evidence told his horrible story before a hushed and incredulous court. Lightning and Lethal were kept in a glass cage for the awe-struck spectators to gaze upon. Once, to highlight an already effervescent trial, Lethal got loose and slithered about the packed room for 10 minutes before she was caught. James, his eyes bulging in fright, leaped up on his chair. Medical testimony stated that the snakebites unquestionably would have killed Mary James in the end, except that their deadly toxic effect was probably weakened by the overdose of drugs.

At one point in the trial the accomplice, who ended up with a life sentence for his role in the murder, stretched himself out flat on the table to demonstrate how he and James had held Mary while they shoved her foot down among the rattlesnakes. James laughed uproariously at the display.

The verdict of guilty was brought in on July 25th and Robert James was sentenced to hang. For the next six years, his attorneys fought the decision, but the sentence was upheld.

Whilst he was awaiting execution, James became a born-again Christian to the fanatical point where he was called "Holy Joe of Death Row."

As the hanging date neared, he asked to talk to reporters.

"Just say I can take it," he told them calmly. "Say that Rattlesnake Bob is not afraid to die. I'm glad to get it over with. My Bible has shown me the way home."

Nina Housden killed her husband then dissected his body. She placed the various parts in boxes and gift wrapped them as Christmas presents. "Charles really wasn't such a bad sort of fellow," she said. "It's just that he ran about with other women"

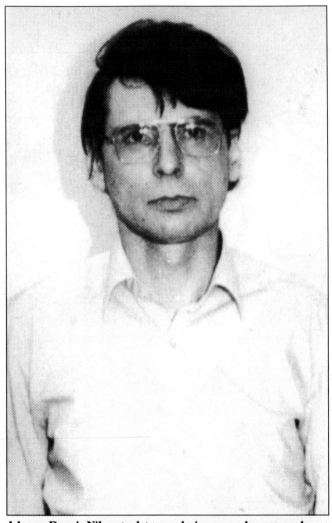

A loner, Dennis Nilsen took to murdering young homosexuals. Their dead bodies provided him with the company he craved. He would later say that it was nice to have someone to come home to, even if it was only a corpse

For Peter Kürten, the famous serial killer known as the Monster of Düsseldorf, sexual pleasure was inextricably linked to blood and death. His victims included men, women, children and even animals

Douglas Daniel Clark would pay prostitutes to have oral sex with him. He would then shoot them in the head and copulate with the corpse. His monstrous partner, Carol Bundy, suggested severing the victims' heads in order to confuse the police

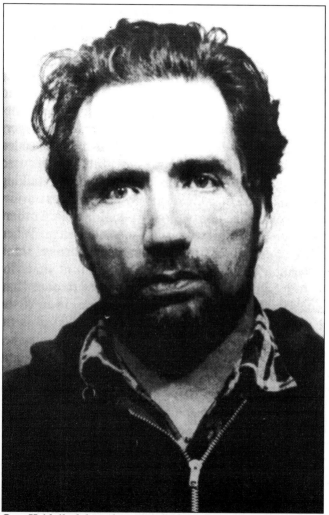

Gary Heidnik abducted women and kept them prisoner in the cellar of his home. They were stripped, chained and forced to satisfy his brutal lust. He claimed that he wanted them to bear his "purified children" away from an impure world

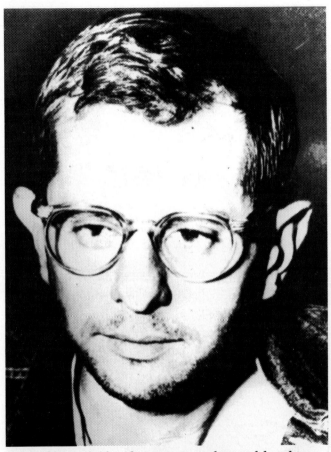

Harvey Glatman's idea of romance was to lure models on bogus photographic assignments, rape them and tie them up as they knelt on the ground. Then he would kill them

Beautiful model Judy Ann Dull was Glatman's first victim

Shirley Ann Bridgeford, an attractive 24-year old brunette divorcee met Glatman through a Lonely Hearts club

Ruth Merardo was forced to spend a day of horror in the desert before Glatman raped and killed her

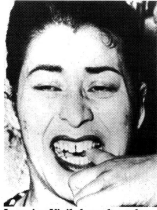

Lorraine Vigil shows how she bit Glatman during her desperate fight for life after being driven down a dark lonely road to be murdered

Glatman's victims

Ruth Ellis and her lover David Blakely. Their violent, mutually destructive affair culminated in her shooting him dead outside a Hampstead pub

9

"MY GOD, SHE'S FINALLY DONE IT!"

"They've killed my husband and they're trying to kill me!" Jackie Lea Floyd's screams shattered the quiet evening calm. Startled neighbours ran outside to see what was going on. They barely recognised the petite brunette who had moved into the exclusive district only a couple of months earlier. Her blouse had been ripped from her body, her face and hands were covered with blood. Tears were streaming down her face and she was shrieking hysterically.

A team of special police investigators from Arkansas arrived at the scene less than 10 minutes later. They entered the house cautiously, fearing that the intruders might still be there. They weren't, but the gruesome consequences of their visit were quickly discovered. Forty-three-year-old Randall Floyd Jr., Jackie Lea's husband, lay face down on the dining-room floor. He was lying in a pool of his own already coagulated blood. His skull had been totally crushed.

Jackie Lea was in a state of shock as she tried to explain to the police what had happened. She said that she and her husband had returned home after visiting some relatives and had surprised two burglars who must have broken into the house while they were away. In the struggle that ensued Jackie's blouse had been torn, her jewellery was ripped from her fingers and she was knocked unconscious. When she came round, she said, she saw her husband lying dead beside her.

Jackie Lea Floyd was clearly distressed, but she was also very concerned how the news would affect her sixteen-year old son, Stormy, currently in town with a friend who had come to visit from Texas. She was expecting him back any moment.

Sure enough, whilst the police where still at the scene, Stormy returned. Told of the burglary and his father's death, the teenager collapsed in grief. His friend, seventeen-year-old David Morgan, did his best to offer comfort, but it didn't do much good. The boy was inconsolable. Evidently he and his father had been very close.

The Floyds had moved to the exclusive district just a couple of months earlier. Randall Floyd was only a truckdriver, but he evidently earned a good living. The place was expensively furnished and decorated with valuable paintings and accessories. Curiously, although the house had been ransacked, the burglars had left many of the expensive items behind. But, of course, being interrupted during their work, they wouldn't have been able to take all they wanted. Still, it was strange that they had evidently taken a number of inexpensive and even worthless items.

As the investigation continued, police began to learn more about the lifestyle of the Floyds. Jackie and Randall, it transpired, had originally been married for seven years, but then they divorced. They had married again just ten months ago, in June 1987, and, though this is not so uncommon, it was evident that they enjoyed a rather unusual relationship.

Randall was hardly ever home, spending most of his time driving across the country earning money to pay the mortgage. In his absence, one of his friends, a fellow truck-driver named Earl Ray Neighbors, had been appointed to be the man about the house. Randall, it appeared, had been concerned about his wife's safety when he was away and had persuaded his friend to move in with them to protect her. According to Neighbors it was an arrangement that neither he nor Jackie relished, but Randall had insisted.

The police were disinclined to stand in judgement of how the victim chose to live. This, after all, was not their job. But it was hard not to think that something was amiss, especially after they found that Mrs Floyd, apart from her two marriages to Randall, had been married no less than five times to other men. Further investigation was clearly called for.

As the inquiry progressed, the police learned that Stormy was not in fact Jackie's son. He was Randall's from an earlier marriage, and had been living with them for only a few months. Previously, he had been living with relatives in Texas and it was not until he got in trouble with the police that Randall had displayed much paternal concern. It was then, after Stormy had been charged with car theft, that Randall had arranged for his son to live with him. "I'll sort him out," he had said. Stormy's friend Morgan had come to Arkansas too. Presumably his family hoped that their boy could be "sorted out" too. Morgan was a drug addict.

Jackie had taken the arrangement in her stride. Though not her natural child, she welcomed Stormy into their home and she was equally gracious to Morgan. But, then again, nothing much ever bothered Jackie Lea Floyd.

Jackie was an insurance salesperson, and very successful she was at it too. She was persuasive, confident and utterly unflappable. People said that Jackie could convince anyone to do anything, or almost.

Jackie believed in insurance and it was a good thing that she did. On November 5th, 1987, the house she and Randall were living in was destroyed by fire. Nearby residents had seen Jackie leave quickly only moments before the fateful explosion. There was some talk of arson, but nothing could be proved and no charges were filed. The fire was attributed to a gas leak and the company with which Jackie was insured duly paid out $50,000.

She used part of the money as down-payment on the present home, furnishing it with the best furniture, appliances and works of art. But, of course, the insurance covered only a fraction of the costs. The remaining mortgage was very high. The repayments were as much as Randall's pay cheque and more, so he took every lorry job he could get, working himself to exhaustion in order to pay for a home he rarely saw.

However, though he didn't have much of a home-life, Randall and Jackie did meet each other at other places. Just a few weeks earlier, for instance, they had met at a truck stop in north Arkansas. There they had talked, reminisced, kissed and cuddled. They also increased their insurance cover. When Jackie said goodbye to her husband that day he was insured for a grand total of $350,000. Jackie, naturally enough, was his sole beneficiary.

By now detectives were firmly convinced that Randall's death was not all that it seemed. But they had no real evidence to disprove the burglary story. Nevertheless, little by little, they began to build up the case for an alternative version. They questioned the relatives that the Floyds had seen that night and learned that Jackie, quite against character, had insisted that they stay the whole evening, whereas on previous visits, she had always wanted to leave as soon she could. Detectives then interviewed the salesman at the jewellery shop where Jackie had bought some of the diamonds that were stolen from her house on the fatal night. They spoke to Randall's friends and relatives. And then they spoke to the guardian of Stormy's young friend, David Morgan. "My God," she said, "she's finally done it!"

Eventually the police uncovered an incredible tale in which David, Earl Ray Neighbors, Jackie Lea and Stormy Floyd had all conspired to murder the luckless truck-

driver. Before the night of March 5th, they had attempted
to kill him on no fewer than four occasions, but, for a
variety of reasons these attempts had failed. Then Jackie
Lea got the idea that a burglary would provide an ideal
pretext for the killing. The fifth and final plot was therefore put into action.

Morgan was to lie in wait for the unsuspecting victim
and batter him to death. He was further instructed to
rough up Jackie in a suitably convincing way, and ran-
sack the house. He would eventually get $10,000 for
those 10 minutes of lethal work.

Morgan bought a baseball bat from a local store, carved
out the head and filled it with lead. Later he showed
detectives where he had sat in the garage preparing the
deadly weapon. A pile of wood shavings was still on the
floor. When Morgan was picked up he made little attempt to hide his guilt. He confessed virtually immediately. "I needed the money for drugs," he said, by way of
explanation.

Stormy Floyd was the second conspirator to be arrested, and faced with Morgan's confession he too admitted his part in the killing. He said he resented his
father trying to control him. Evidently his stepmother
had fanned that resentment into hatred until he was
ready to kill. He recalled how they plotted constantly
about the best way to kill Randall and collect the insurance money.

Jackie Lea Floyd was later picked up at the hospital
where she was still receiving treatment for her minor
injuries. Faced with the evidence against her, she admitted her part in the plot and said that it had been a long
time in the making. She hated her husband, she said,
and though the poor fool thought that she was in love
with him again when they remarried, she had hated him
even on their wedding night.

Jackie said that she and Earl Ray Neighbors had met
during her separation from Randall and they had become
lovers and conspirators on almost the same night. She

knew that Randall would be happy to marry her again, and she knew too that he would readily agree to be insured. If the plan had worked, Jackie declared, then she would have become a very rich widow and she and Earl Ray would have lived a life of bliss.

Even in these troubled times, Jackie Lea's callous treatment of her husband stands out as particularly horrific and neither she nor her lover expected to receive much sympathy in the courtroom. They were not disappointed.

In September 1988 Jackie Lea Floyd and David Morgan were sentenced to life in prison with no chance of parole. Earl Ray Neighbors got 25 years for solicitation to commit murder and Stormy Floyd was sentenced to 30 years for his part in the murder of his father.

10

HE WORE HIS VICTIM
ON HIS CHEST

On October 9th, 1988, Jesus Sanchez telephoned the police in Portland, Maine, saying he thought a young woman he knew was hurt or even dead. He gave them his address and awaited their arrival.

Shortly afterwards, Sanchez was explaining to Detective James Beecher why he believed a man named Ricardo Cruz had killed Jessica Woodley, a cocaine addict he had known for some time. Cruz had been her dealer, said Sanchez, but there were many others who supplied her with the drugs she craved. Jessica would do anything for a snort of cocaine, he said, producing a pile of photographs to illustrate what he meant. Beecher quickly grasped what he meant. The pictures all showed the same young woman in various states of undress.

Sanchez said that he had been with Ricardo Cruz at Jessica's apartment the previous evening. They had a few drinks and then Cruz and Jessica had started arguing. Sanchez decided it was time to leave. He went outside to hail a cab, but after 10 minutes he gave up and returned to the apartment.

Cruz was sitting at the kitchen table, but Jessica was nowhere in sight. Sanchez said he tried to go into her bedroom, but Cruz blocked his path. Sanchez decided to stay in the apartment overnight and lay down on the couch. Cruz remained awake. Not once did he catch sight or sound of Jessica.

As Sanchez continued with his story, the voice of Cruz was heard on the pavement outside. Beecher looked out of the window and saw the man pacing up and down the street. He was clearly disturbed and very agitated.

Cruz then stripped off his T-shirt to reveal three pictures of a naked woman that were taped to his chest. Shouting in Spanish, Cruz then put his finger to his throat, miming the action of a throat being cut.

Officers rushed to Jessica Woodley's apartment. They found her dead body on the bedroom floor. Beside her lay a leather belt.

Cruz was arrested and charged with the intentional murder of Jessica Woodley. At his trial the jury learned that Ricardo Cruz had become incensed with the woman he regarded as his own property being supplied by other dealers and trading sex for drugs. Eventually he decided he would stand it no more. He placed a blanket around her throat and then used her belt to choke her.

Ricardo Cruz was found guilty and, on August 2nd, 1990, he was sentenced to 45 years' imprisonment.

11

BIRTHDAY KILLER

In the early morning of May 16th, 1971, Patricia Sils was found strangled in a roadside ditch on the outskirts of North Chicago. There was no sign of a struggle and no clues to be found, but whoever killed her had screwed up her stockings and suspender belt and stuffed them down inside her slacks.It was as if the killer had dressed her when she was dead, but had overlooked this last detail.

An interview with her husband convinced the investigators that James Sils was not responsible for the killing. However, their marriage was on the rocks and Patricia used to stay away from home at weekends. She was a drinker, and hung around bars picking up other men. Detectives made a round of all the local bars, asking questions until they found a bartender who knew Patricia Sils and remembered the man she had been with that last evening. He was a sailor who had bought a round of drinks for everybody. The barman described the man, and said his largesse was due to the fact that he had been celebrating his birthday.

Now the police really had something. They were looking for a killer whose birthday was on May 15th. Over the next three days they checked military files until they came up with recent transfers whose birthdays fell on that date. One name fitted perfectly: Guy Thomas Fricano.

When Fricano was picked up he admitted being with Patricia Sils that Saturday and leaving the bar at the same time. He said her car pulled out first, but once on the road she stopped in front of him. Fricano said he pulled up beside her and asked if she was going to another bar. Patricia said she was and invited him to come along too.

The sailor said that when they stopped at the second bar the barmaid refused to serve Patricia, so he suggested that they go to a motel where they could mix their own drinks. Patricia agreed. They left her car at the tavern and went in his car to the Pagoda Motel. Once in their room, Fricano said, they stripped off. Then Patricia decided she didn't want sex. She also said her drink was too strong.

"I told her to mix her own," he said. "But instead of doing that, she took the bottle of liquor and poured it all down the wash basin. Then she laughed about it."

To this point the officers believed Fricano's story. But they did not believe the sailor's account of what happened next.

Fricano said he became very angry and ordered her to return to his car. Then, he said, he took her back into town and told her to get out. He had not seen her since.

Three months later, however, Fricano revised his statement. Instead of taking her into town, Fricano said, he became angry with her and strangled her with her own stockings. He said he had put her clothes back on the body but had forgotten the stockings and suspender belt, so he rolled them into a ball and stuffed them into her slacks. He then dumped the body out of his car.

In 1972 Guy Thomas Fricano pleaded guilty to the charge that he murdered Patricia Sils. He claimed that if someone had remembered his birthday he would not have felt the same way. Patricia would still be alive.

12

THE DE KAPLANY CASE

Dr Geza de Kaplany was a Hungarian refugee and something of a ladies' man. In 1962, whilst working as an anaesthetist at a hospital in San Jose, California, he met a ravishing model who, though sixteen years his junior, he courted with a passion. They married in August, and soon Geza and Hajna were setting up home in a new apartment block across town.

The marriage was a happy one, at least for the first few days. But then, within a week of moving into their new home, things started to go wrong. Dr de Kaplany found himself impotent and quite unable to make love to his beautiful wife. What Hajna may have said about this remains unknown, but de Kaplany quickly developed paranoid fantasies about her. He convinced himself that all the men in the apartment block were having affairs with her, and that she was encouraging them.

On August 28th, 1962, residents in the area were disturbed by the loud music coming from the de Kaplany apartment. They could also hear a woman's piercing screams above the din. After repeatedly banging on the walls and knocking on the door without getting any response, his neighbours finally decided to call the police. About an hour later the police arrived.

The officers banged on de Kaplany's front door until the music suddenly stopped. Then the door swung open.

Before them stood the doctor, grinning madly and dressed only in bloodstained underwear, his hands covered with rubber gloves. On the bed lay Hajna, naked and horribly mutilated.

Dr de Kaplany had stripped her and tied her hands and feet to the bedposts. He had then made small incisions all over her body, into which he had poured sulphuric, hydrochloric and nitric acids. He had ignored her screams of agony, merely turning up the volume of the stereo a little higher whenever she yelled. He had then systematically mutilated Hajna's face, her breasts and her genitals, slashing and cutting at her with a scalpel. He hadn't wanted to kill her, he later explained, only spoil her good looks.

Hajna de Kaplany lingered in agony in hospital for over a month before she finally died. Her husband was charged with her murder.

He pleaded not guilty by reason of insanity and described the episode as "my one-hour crack-up".

In court de Kaplany remained calm and composed until the prosecution displayed photographs of his victim. The doctor then became hysterical. "I loved her! If I did this – and I must have done this – then I am guilty!"

On March 1st, 1963 Dr Geza de Kaplany was found guilty and sentenced to life imprisonment.

For reasons that have never been explained Dr de Kaplany was released twelve years later. He was smuggled out of America in 1975 and sent to the Far East. It was said that his expertise as a "cardiac specialist" was vital to a Taiwan missionary hospital. Oddly, however, de Kaplany was never a specialist in heart medicine.

13

LINDA PARALYSED HER LOVER

It was just after 12 o'clock on May 28th, 1992, when the California police took the frantic call from Linda Phillips. She was hysterical and screaming but between her sobs the police were able to make out that there had been a shooting. The caller's ex-boyfriend had apparently broken into a house and got violent. A gun had gone off.

Detectives soon arrived at the Phillips' luxury home. Linda was standing outside the house, sobbing. "I shot him in the head," she blurted out. "He's upstairs."

The officers dashed upstairs to the master bedroom. There they were met by a team of paramedics who were already attending to the victim. The man, later identified as Ricardo Ornelas, was lying flat on his back on the floor, his face a blood-caked mess. He was dressed in blue trousers, the tattered remains of a white dress shirt and black shoes. The front of his shirt was torn away and his vest had been cut open by the paramedics. One of the bullets had knocked out four of his teeth.

Streaks of crimson trailed down the white cupboard a few feet away. It was there where the victim had initially been discovered, propped up in a grotesque repose. A white wicker chair lay on its side near the body.

There were some blood spots in the centre of the rumpled eiderdown. On the floor at the foot of the bed, partially protruding from under the eiderdown, was a Smith & Wesson .38-calibre revolver.

Linda Phillips was in no fit state to talk but she was taken to the police station for questioning.

She told the officers that she and Ricardo Ornelas has been dating for about a year. They had broken up in February, but Ricardo had phoned her twice that morning begging to have lunch with her. She had refused. Then, at about noon, he had forced his way into the house, and had come up to the bedroom.

Having heard stories of lovers' disputes a hundred times before, the officers had no reason to doubt Linda's emotional account of the confrontation. They listened carefully as she tearfully continued.

Ricardo had been angry, she said. Her voice trembled as she described how he had pulled out the gun and yelled, "I'm going to kill you first, and then myself!" She was terribly frightened. When Ricardo put the weapon down, and sat on a couch next to the bed, Linda leapt up and grabbed it. Then there was a "terrible accident".

Ricardo stood up and cried out as he lunged towards her. Terrified he was going to attack her, she fired again, and he fell to the floor. Panic-stricken, Linda had then phoned the police.

It seemed like a straightforward story. But as the enquiry progressed, a number of things failed to add up. Ornelas had recently left his family to live with his ex-maid, so it seemed odd that he should now be chasing an old flame. And the same day as he had visited Linda Phillips, Ornelas had made an application for vision-care insurance. Why should a man intent on murder and suicide trouble about his eyesight? Then there was the gun. It wasn't stolen, it didn't belong to Ornelas and it was 50 years old. None of these things seemed to make any sense.

A check into the background of Linda Phillips perplexed detectives still further. She had been arrested several times in the past for writing bogus cheques and for forgery. She had served time in prison for fraud. Included in her record were no fewer than 25 aliases she had used, along with eight different Social Security numbers. Linda had listed three different ages, ranging from 35 upwards. Her unblemished skin, bright eyes and stunning figure made her seem ageless. But 35 seemed too young. In fact, as detectives later learned, she was already 50.

By now the police were certain that Linda's story was a fiction. Friends of hers were already telling them about her vengeful character. "Everything's fine if you go along with her," one said, "but if you cross her, watch out." Nobody seemed in any doubt that the lady was quite capable of violence. Furthermore, the detectives also learned of Linda's jealousy when Ornelas dropped her in favour of his maid. She was furious, witnesses said, when Ornelas left his family to live with his new lover. He had often promised to move in with her, but these promises had always come to nothing.

Certain though they were, however, they needed something a great deal more concrete before they could make an arrest and bring the case to court. Try as they might, however, no hard evidence emerged.

But then the police had a stroke of luck. They tracked down a friend of Linda, a certain Marshall Cochrane, to a half-way house for released convicts in Tampa, Florida. It was he who had supplied the gun.

"I bought Linda a gun for her self-protection," Cochrane admitted.

"Where did you get it?" asked the officers.

"From a guy in Santa Ana."

"When?"

Cochrane remembered that he had acquired the revolver in the first week of May. Shown a picture of the Smith & Wesson that had shot Ornelas, he identified it as the same gun.

Linda Phillips was picked up later that day. Faced with

the new evidence, she admitted that the .38 belonged to her. The true story, she revealed, was that Ornelas had forced his way into the house and threatened her while yelling that he was going to commit suicide. He was always whining about killing himself, she said, so she decided to call his bluff. She put the revolver down on the couch, implying that if he wanted to kill himself, there was the gun.

She was surprised, she said, when he picked the weapon up and aimed it at her. They struggled and the gun fell to the floor. She managed to get her hands on it, and just when she picked it up it fired, hitting him in the back of the head. But apparently he hadn't been badly wounded, because he then lunged at her. Her hands were shaking so badly that she pulled the trigger again. That is when he fell to the floor.

Detectives listened patiently to the new version and then, when she had finished, they told Linda Phillips that she was under arrest.

"What do you mean?" she howled, "You can't be serious!"

At her trial the jury heard how Linda Phillips had lured Ornelas to her home to kill him. She had shot him twice and let him lie helplessly with a damaged spinal cord that made him a quadriplegic while he slowly and painfully bled to death.

Following five days of deliberation, Linda Phillips was found guilty of second-degree murder. She didn't take the verdict mildly. Standing, she loudly berated the court, the trial and the prosecution. She sacked her lawyer, refusing to speak to him.

She is still angry now and, behind the bars of the state prison, she is likely to remain angry for a very long time.

14

HE LIVED WITH HIS LOVER'S HEADLESS CORPSE

The stench from the caravan was overwhelming. It was so bad that the police called the fire brigade. Before they ventured inside they wanted the fire-fighters to use pressurised gas and force out the stagnant foul air. The fire brigade came and did their work, but it was of limited effect. The putrid odour still remained. It was a bright spring morning in 1989 and everyone who was there felt sick.

The caravan had been the home of 40-year-old Marilyn Griffin and her boyfriend, Brian Daly, a man twelve years her junior. They had lived in the caravan park near Orlando airport, Florida, for about seven months and though none of their neighbours knew them well, they had all heard the couple's shouts. The two were always fighting.

The arguments had reached a peak in February and had prompted the park keeper to come over and see what was going on. Brian wasn't in when he called, but Marilyn was. She tried her best to cover up the evidence of their rows, but it was a pointless task. There was so much damage to the caravan that it just couldn't be hidden. Windows were broken and a door to the front bedroom had a hole in it.

The tearful woman broke down and wept. She admitted to the keeper that her boyfriend had been beating her and making her life hell. He broke all her furniture in his fits of anger, she said. Marilyn was petrified lest he heard about the visit; she was sure it would lead to yet another row. But the keeper insisted that something would have to be done.

As it turned out, however, no more action was needed for the rows soon stopped. After the keeper's visit there were no more shouts and screams from their caravan. In fact, all was deadly quiet. Brian Daly was seen going in and out of the caravan and was, apparently, in good humour. Marilyn wasn't seen, but her absence wasn't noticed. And then the smell started.

As detectives entered the mobile home, the bathroom door stood open, allowing a clear view of a bloodstained human head lying in the sink. On the floor of the bedroom adjacent to the bathroom lay a headless human body. Blood and brain matter was everywhere. Marilyn Griffin had been decapitated by the blast of a shotgun. Her body, which had been there for some time, was crawling with maggots.

It didn't take long to track down Marilyn's boyfriend. He was found drinking in a bar where she had worked. Detectives asked if everything was OK. He said, "Everything except I'm screwed up in the head."

At the trial it was established that Marilyn Griffin had been planning to leave him. Daly, true to character, lashed out and then fired the shotgun. He then carried on living in the caravan even as her corpse was rotting.

Brian Patrick Daly was indicted on charges of first-degree murder but was allowed a plea of guilty to the lesser charge of murder in the second degree. On August 21st, 1989, he was sentenced to 22 years' imprisonment.

15
THE SPOILT BRAT ROMEO

In almost everyone's estimation Vincent Gonzales was a spoilt brat. His parents, who were separated, indulged his every whim. There was not a thing they denied him. Eventually, however, the boy's appetite for getting his own way proved too much for even them. In July 1992 he and his father had a massive row.

Vincent had been accused of stealing a gun from the firm where both he and his father worked. He denied the crime, of course, but his father was not convinced. Moreover, the episode served to remind Gonzales Senior of all the other times his son had lied. He decided there and then that he would tolerate it no more. Throwing Vincent out of his house he vowed he would have nothing to do with him again.

Not unnaturally, Vincent was upset by this change in his fortunes. He didn't mope about it, though. Instead he went round to his girlfriend's house in New Rochdale, New York, and told her family his tale of woe.

Vincent had been going out with eighteen-year-old Lucy Malacria for almost three months and knew her family to be kind and supportive. He was certain that they would understand his awful predicament. In this, he was not disappointed.

The Malacria family took the errant 19-year-old under their wing. They fed him, housed him, even bought him clothes, and when the Malacrias went on holiday to Italy Vincent went along too, with his girlfriend's family picking up most of the bills.

After a while, however, the Malacrias began to feel Vincent was taking advantage of them. Lucy's father was particularly annoyed when, without bothering to ask permission, Vincent drove away in his car. And then there was the time that they caught him stealing from one of their friends. As long as Lucy remained keen on him they allowed the situation to ride. But, when she too began to cool they decided that it was time for things to end. On Wednesday, September 9th, Vincent Gonzales was shown the door.

The dejected boy returned to his mother's house. Complaining of a fever he told her he was feeling awful. He said he was going to kill himself. Mrs Gonzales tried to be sympathetic, but she found it hard to take the lad seriously. He moped about the house for two days. Then, on Friday evening Vincent told his mother he had to collect some of his things from Lucy.

Vincent met Lucy that evening at the home of one of her friends. The first shot went wild. The next hit its mark. Lucy Malacria, injured, fell to the ground. Vincent Gonzales now turned the gun to his own face and pulled the trigger. He collapsed near to where his ex-girlfriend lay.

At first it was assumed that the two teenagers had both been the victims of a crazed attack, but soon the truth came out. Lucy's condition continued to deteriorate and six days later she died. On October 5th, 1992, still recovering in a hospital bed, Victor Gonzales was charged with murder.

Gonzales was found guilty of manslaughter on November 30th, 1992. He was sentenced to a minimum of 15 years' imprisonment.

16

"WHAT WE DID TO JAMIE"

Fourteen and fond of flirting, Darla Jo Swinford was trouble. It would have been better for three teenage boys if they had never met her. Better, especially, for 18-year-old Jamie Medlin. Dating Darla cost him his life.

Jamie lived in Southaven, near Memphis, Tennessee, and it was there on December 29th, 1990, that a trucker driving along a lonely stretch of road saw the young man's dead body, his face obliterated by a gaping wound. Death had been caused by a single shotgun blast to the mouth.

Jamie Medlin had started dating Darla Jo in November when her regular boyfriend, 18-year-old George Johnson, was away in Orlando. Darla Jo had used his absence to play the field and Medlin was soon under her spell.

Jamie's relatives were worried that Swinford was just dating him to make Johnson jealous. George Johnson was a troubled youth and his violent temper was well known. Perhaps, they thought, Darla was hoping to convince him that leaving her for so long was a mistake. In the event, however, what was going through Darla's mind was something far darker. She wasn't merely playing with the boy's affections, she was playing with his life.

It was in a diner a few weeks later that Darla was overheard talking to Johnson, who had now come back from his holiday. The gist of the conversation was that they were planning to shoot the young boy. It is still unclear whether it was Johnson or Darla who first came up with the notion. But once it was raised, they both fell in with the plan.

A date was arranged for Darla to ask Medlin to take her to a diner. After dinner she persuaded him to go for an evening drive. It probably didn't take much convincing on Darla's part to get Medlin to stop on the deserted road.

At about 9 p.m. Johnson and a friend, Richard Barnum, arrived on the scene. While Darla waited inside the car, Medlin and Johnson stood and argued in the street. The words became increasingly harsh and accusatory. But all dialogue ended abruptly when Johnson pulled out a shotgun and brought Medlin to the rear of his car. Johnson then placed the barrel against Medlin's mouth and squeezed the trigger.

During the six months in prison awaiting her trial, Darla Jo Swinford exchanged letters with Johnson. Intercepted by prison officials, the letters showed a girlish scrawl revealing both intent and a little remorse in one line: "Isn't it terrible what we did to Jamie?"

George Johnson and Richard Barnum both agreed to plead guilty. As a result, both received life sentences. For conspiracy to commit murder Johnson got an additional 20 years.

Darla Jo too was found guilty and she also was sentenced to imprisonment for life.

17
LISA AND LORI

Lisa Cihaski's body was found slumped in the front seat of her car in the early hours of September 22nd, 1989. Her neck was swollen and livid. She had been strangled.

There was no indication of a sexual assault and the motive had not been robbery. The police at Wassau, Wisconsin were thus left to find a more personal motive and murderer. But who would have wanted to kill the twenty-one-year-old former high-school beauty queen? Lisa was a popular girl. She wasn't the type to have enemies.

Lisa had recently got engaged and her fiancé was one of the first people the police interviewed. Already they suspected that her forthcoming marriage held the key to her death. Could the murderer have been an old suitor, perhaps, or a rival for her affections?

Lisa had many friends, both male and female, and they were all questioned. But no one emerged as a likely suspect. No one, that is, until Lori Esker came into the picture. She wasn't Lisa's friend, but she had known her fiancé. She was his old girlfriend.

Lori made no effort to disguise the fact that she had been upset when her boyfriend left her for Lisa. She had been even more upset when the engagement was announced. But she denied taking her anger out on the girl.

As the interrogation continued, however, and Lori's alibis became more and more suspect, the woman finally confessed. "I did it!" she blurted out. "I killed her, but it was self-defence. I thought she was going to kill me."

Lori went on to tell the police of her relationship with Lisa Cihaski's fiancé. She said they had been a perfect couple and had even been talking about marriage. And then he told her he was planning to marry Lisa.

"I was devastated," sobbed Lori. "I tried to think of some way I could break them up, and then it occurred to me. I would tell Lisa I was pregnant."

Lori met Lisa outside the motel where she worked and they both got into Lisa's car. Then Lori delivered her news. It was then, according to Lori, that Lisa went wild. "She became angry and started to call me names, and then grabbed me by the throat. I thought she was going to kill me."

Lori said that during the struggle she found a belt on the car seat and she put it around her rival's neck. She pushed Lisa down and "held the belt tight until Lisa went limp". "It was scary," Lori said. "I just sat there for a while, not knowing if she was dead or had just passed out. I took a mirror from my handbag and held it to her mouth. She wasn't breathing and I knew she was dead, but I really didn't mean to kill her. All I wanted was for her not to marry my man."

Lori Esker's trial began on June 7th, 1990. She was charged with first-degree, intentional murder, the prosecution arguing that even if the crime was not long-planned, Lori must have held the belt for some minutes, during which she was acting with premeditation.

It was a questionable legal point but one which the jury evidently accepted. They found Lori Esker guilty of first-degree murder, which under Wisconsin law carries a mandatory life sentence.

18
ARSON FOR THE BRIDE

It had been a big night. The party at the Buck home on the edge of Marion, Pennsylvania, had gone on right into the small hours. Everyone had had a marvellous time. The New Year, 1937, had been properly launched.

Now it was a little after 3 o'clock and the last of the revellers were making their way home. Suddenly, from the house next door came a dull, booming roar, followed instantly by screams and the light of raging flames.

Jaime Martin leapt from the porch and raced across the snow to the burning home 100 yards away. When he reached there a minute later the place was an inferno. He tried the front door, but it was locked. Darting towards the rear of the house, he saw the swaying silhouette of a girl behind one of the ground floor windows. He easily recognised her as Catherine Gelwix, the 21-year-old daughter of the household.

Without hesitating, he shattered the window and crashed into the room. He caught the girl as she collapsed and carried her out to safety.

By now the fire brigade were on their way. But there was precious little they would be able to do. The house and its occupants were doomed.

How many were inside? Two for sure: Catherine's mother and her 15-year-old sister, Helen Louise. And there might have been a third: Catherine's fiancé, a young fellow by the name of Ralph Hawk.

By the time police investigators had arrived on the scene the house was destroyed. Only a smouldering ruin remained. It had happened so quickly no one was left in any doubt that the fire had been started deliberately. Moreover, the police had other reasons for suspecting foul play. Catherine Gelwix was now in hospital, but she wasn't just being treated for burns and shock. She had also sustained an injury to her head. Before the fire had started someone had struck her.

It had been a nasty blow but doctors were hopeful she would make a full recovery. Her mother and younger sister were not so fortunate. They had both perished in the flames. Thankfully, Catherine's boyfriend, Ralph, had not been in the house.

Ralph Hawk heard about the fire just before Sheriff Charles Gillan arrived at the farm where he worked.

"How's Catherine?" he asked. "We just heard. I'm on my way to the hospital now."

"She'll be all right," replied the sheriff sympathetically. "But I do want to ask a few questions. It will only take a moment. We understand you visited Catherine last night."

"Yes, sir. We were talking over last-minute plans for the wedding."

"What time did you leave?"

"Right after the whistles blew at midnight."

"Why did you leave so early?"

"I was taking a chance as it was," explained Hawk. "My licence expired yesterday and I didn't have new plates. I knew you fellows were picking up cars with old tags so I got off the road as fast as I could."

"What time did you get home?"

Hawk looked at his boss. "I don't know exactly," he replied. "I didn't look at the clock. But it's only a half-hour's drive to Catherine's place. It couldn't have been much after one."

"That's right," said Hawk's boss. "I heard him come in."

"Can I go now?" asked Hawk nervously. "I want to get to the hospital."

The sheriff nodded. The young man's nervousness was understandable and his answers had been simple and straightforward. And his story had been verified by his boss.

"Go ahead," he said. "Maybe you'll help that poor girl pull through."

Once Hawk had left, the sheriff asked his boss a few more questions. The man clearly liked his employee and thought him to be a sensible and trustworthy young man. Furthermore, he could see Ralph was desperately in love with Catherine.

"Why, you should have seen the ring he gave her for Christmas," he exclaimed. "It must have set him back plenty."

"You mean an engagement ring?" asked the Gillan.

"No, it was just a present. Extravagant, it was. I saw it on his dresser one morning. He became kind of flustered when I said it must have cost a lot of money. But he said that nothing was too good for Catherine."

Gillan was deep in thought as he went back to his car. It was strange that he had seen no ring on the girl's finger. Surely she would have been wearing it?

As it turned out, the sheriff had never been curious about a more important matter. For as he questioned Catherine later that day, he learned the surprising fact that Hawk had never given her a ring, engagement or otherwise.

"I didn't want him to," she explained with a tender smile. "I thought it best we save our money to set up house."

Early the next morning police started on a round of the

local jewellery stores and found the shop where a sales-man remembered the sale of a lady's ring to Ralph Hawk. He had records to prove it. The transaction had taken place a few days before Christmas.

"Do you know who the ring was for?" asked the sheriff.

"Why, yes, I do," replied the jeweller. "The day after Christmas the young lady came in to have the band made smaller. It was the Borger girl, Betty Borger."

A short time later Sheriff Gillan made a visit to Miss Borger's home. She was a very attractive girl, and as the sheriff started to question her her large brown eyes were wide with curiosity. Gillan gazed at the exquisite ring on the third finger of the girl's left hand.

"I understand," he began carefully, "that Ralph Hawk gave you that ring."

Miss Borger smiled, held up her hand and gazed admiringly at the jewelled circlet. "Yes," she said. "Isn't it lovely?"

"It is indeed," agreed the sheriff. "It must have set him back a lot of money."

The girl flushed and dropped her hand. "It's our engagement ring," she said with a proud lift of her head.

"Engagement ring?" Gillan exclaimed. "Didn't you know he was already engaged to another girl?"

Miss Borger paled.

"Another girl? That's impossible."

The sheriff shook his head sadly. "I'm afraid not. He was engaged to that girl who was burned in the fire New Year's Eve, Catherine Gelwix. They were to have been married yesterday. But now, since the fire, and the death of Catherine's mother and sister, I imagine the wedding has been postponed. It was lucky that Catherine didn't die in the fire too."

Slowly, as the sheriff spoke the colour drained from the girl's face. It was clear that she had caught the hidden meaning of his words. "I don't want to hear any more," she said in a shocked voice.

Swiftly she twisted the ring from her finger and dropped it into Gillan's palm. "Here. Take it. Give it back to him. Tell him I never want to see him again."

Gillan tucked the ring away in his pocket.

Ralph Hawk put up a good front when he was ushered into the sheriff's office that afternoon. "I saw Catherine this morning," he said with a confident smile. "She's coming along fine. We'll be able to get married after all."

"I don't know about that," said Gillan. "There are a few things that you have to clear up first."

"What do you mean?" the young man asked.

"Well," replied the sheriff, "maybe you'd better start off with this."

Sheriff Gillan took out the ring from his pocket and placed it on the table.

Hawk caught his breath.

"Where did you get that?" he asked.

"From the girl you gave it to a week before you were to marry Catherine."

The sheriff's voice became hard. "Is that why you tried to kill Catherine? Because you had fallen for Betty Borger?"

"No. No," said Hawk.

Gillan's fist hit the desk. "You're lying."

"No. I love Catherine."

"Yet you gave the other girl an expensive ring, just a week before your wedding."

"Betty and I were just friends."

"That's not the way she tells it."

With an effort Hawk got a grip on himself. "I know it looks bad for me," he said. "But you've got to believe me. I love Cathy. I tried to get her to move up the date of our wedding."

"It won't wash," snapped Gillan. "That was part of the alibi you were building up before the crime. You got yourself engaged to two girls at the same time and the only way out you could see was murder."

Hawk suddenly slumped forward in his chair. "Yes," he said in a choked voice. "I was mad."

Later that day Hawk dictated a detailed confession. He had left Catherine's house shortly after midnight on New Year's Eve on the pretext of visiting his father but with the promise of returning shortly. Catherine was to have left the door open for him. However, he had not returned until just before 3 o'clock. He had deliberately waited until Catherine would have given up hope of his return and, like her mother and sister, retired to bed. A quick survey of the house had showed him that all lights were out before he stealthily entered the unlocked door. It had taken but a matter of seconds to get the kerosene can from its place by the kitchen stove and douse the two bedrooms with the explosive fluid. Just before he had struck the fatal match Catherine had sat up in bed. It was then that he had struck her down.

Two people had burned to death in the fire he had started. And on March 28th, 1939, Ralph Hawk also burned: in the electric chair in the State Penitentiary at Bellefonte, Pennsylvania.

19
POISONED CHOCOLATES

Oddvar Eiken, a student at Lund Medical College, Sweden, glanced inquisitively at the small package that eight-year-old Marianne Svennson, daughter of his landlady, had just brought into his apartment. Although the name and address of the sender was missing, a broad smile flashed across his face when he noticed that the postmark was Kristiansand, Norway.

"It's from your sister Randi," he called out to his room-mate Anders Muren as he removed the wrapping-paper. Inside were four chocolates, each piece packed separately in a matchbox. There was also a white gift card signed Randi. She told him to eat all the chocolates himself.

"Isn't that just like a woman!" Anders exclaimed in mock indignation. "My own sister denying me a chocolate. And I'm the one who brought you two together!"

In love though he was, Oddvar disregarded his fiancée's order. He gave a chocolate to Marianne, who in turn shared it with her friend Barbro. He also gave one to Oddvar.

Early next morning the house was awakened by Marianne's screams. The pretty little girl had been seized with violent cramps and nausea. A short time later Oddvar and Anders were also stricken. So too was Barbro. All four were rushed to a nearby hospital, where it was discovered that they had been poisoned. Special stomach washes were administered, but despite all the hospital's efforts, little Marianne slipped into a coma and died. The other three managed to recover.

Not surprisingly, it was discovered that Randi Muren had never sent any chocolates to her boyfriend.

After a prolonged police investigation, which involved the forces of Denmark, Norway and Sweden, the true culprit was identified as Carstein Brekke, a student friend of Randi Muren and a boy who held a secret passion for the girl. He thought that secretly she loved him too.

In his subsequent confession Brekke said that Randi had given him a letter to post to Oddvar Eiken and he had opened the seal and read it. When he saw that she had started her letter "My dear husband," he was stunned. "Something inside me snapped," he said.

It was then that he decided on the plan to send poisoned chocolates to Oddvar Eiken and make out they came from Randi. This plot, he thought, would serve the duel purpose of killing his rival and punishing his love.

Brekke was put on trial in late October 1949 and promptly retracted his earlier confession. Though he still admitted sending the poisoned chocolates, he now claimed that his purpose was simply to make Eiken ill and that he hoped she would blame Randi and break off their engagement.

He was charged with the attempted premeditated murder of Oddvar Eiken and with the manslaughter of little Marianne Svennson. The jury deliberated for two hours before returning their verdict.

The majority decision was that he was guilty, and Carstein Brekke was thus sentenced to 12 years' imprisonment and 10 years' loss of his rights as a citizen. On appeal his sentence was increased by a further three years.

20
BATTERED TO DEATH

It was only a few months after their marriage in 1890
that Edwyn and Emily Shears realised they weren't made
for each other. In the years that followed, things didn't
improve. They developed a mutual dislike which steadily
drove them further and further apart. By the time they
were in their fifties, they had more or less gone their
separate ways, Emily concerning herself mostly with her
three children and Edwyn devoting his spare time to the
garden of their Bournemouth home.

Yet whilst it was clear that Edwyn had long since
stopped loving his wife, he was still jealous. Whenever
Emily went out by herself she would return home to find
her husband accusing her of "manhunting" and all sorts
of infidelity. These arguments would often end in violence, and Emily had the bruises to prove it.

Such a marriage would not have lasted long in modern times, but in those days people stayed together, regardless of how bad things might be. So the Shearses'
marriage endured... until the evening of November 19th,
1934.

There was a film showing locally that Emily wanted to
see. She told her husband where she was going, but he
took little interest, preoccupied as he was with cement-
ing some brickwork on the garden path. But when Emily
returned home later that night Edwyn was furious.

"Where have you been?" he asked roughly.

Annoyed by his words, and possibly inspired by the crisp dialogue of the film she had just seen, Emily taunted him by saying that she had indeed on this occasion been out "manhunting". Incensed, Edwyn threw a bucket of water over her.

In panic, the drenched wife leapt over the rockery, followed by her husband, who was muttering, "I will kill you." She then stooped to pick up a brick and launched it at Edwyn, who fell to the ground. A neighbour heard a thud and moaning and, his suspicions aroused, called the police.

When the police arrived Emily was covering her husband with a coat. "When I returned home just now I found him like this," she said.

"Has he been fighting with anyone?" asked one of the policemen.

"I shouldn't be surprised. He is a bastard of a man." As he was carried into the house Emily ventured: "He's been plastering. I expect he fell down." The sergeant noted the serious wounds in his head – six in all. And it didn't look like an accident.

Later, Emily confessed to the deed. But she said she had done it in self-defence. "If he had got hold of me he would have killed me," she said.

Arrested on a murder charge, Emily Shears was taken to Holloway Prison and eventually brought to trial. In the witness box she spoke of her unhappy life with her husband and the years of violence and humiliation.

The jury found her guilty of manslaughter, and the judge, sensing she was neither a hardened criminal nor a vicious person, pronounced a sentence of 12 months' imprisonment. It was the price she was willing to pay for freedom from a brutal husband. At least Emily Shears' remaining years could be lived in peace.

21

SHALLOW GRAVE FOR A BRUTAL HUSBAND

Bill Pierce's tearful wife told the officers at the station in Jacksonville, Arkansas, that her husband hadn't been home since Saturday. Lisa Pierce said they had been out in the evening and drunk far too much. Then Bill had gone to the cemetery to visit his mother's grave and she had gone home. She hadn't seen him since.

The police made the usual routine calls. They spoke to Bill's family and friends. They also checked the local hospitals, but the man was nowhere to be found. Ten days later, however, he was discovered. Bill Pierce's decaying body was found in a shallow grave on land owned by 22-year-old George Justin Solida, a slow-witted individual who was also an alcoholic and one of Bill's old friends.

After Solida was arrested and charged with the murder he broke down and confessed the full story. He said he had been involved in a torrid affair with Bill's wife which had grown hotter with each passionate encounter. He eventually proposed marriage. Lisa did not believe in divorce, he said, but she did believe in murder. And the fact that her husband was well insured aided her in this faith.

Solida claimed that Lisa had already made one attempt to kill her husband. She had put poison in his beer. That attempt failed dismally, however, as it had only made him vomit. The pair now decided it would be better to hire a professional to do the deed. Alas, this plan also failed. And so it was that, on July 12th, 1987 Solida resolved to do the killing himself.

Bill, he said, was so drunk he didn't know what was happening. Solida carried him into his car and drove him to his home. It was there, said Solida, that he had taken out his rifle and shot his friend in the chest. Bill Pierce died instantly.

"I tried to bury him, but the ground was too hard and rocky and I couldn't dig a hole," the killer explained. Instead Solida wrapped his victim in an old blanket and drove him to where the ground was softer and far easier to dig. But by now dawn was already breaking and there was only time to dig a grave two feet deep.

Lisa Pierce denied all knowledge of the conspiracy. She insisted on her love for her husband and was adamant about her fidelity. Only when a registration slip from a motel proved that she had spent the night with Solida did Lisa admit that she had indeed been unfaithful. She then began a litany of complaints about her brutal husband to justify her behaviour.

Finally she admitted that she had also been involved in her husband's murder. She said that she had been present when he was shot, but she swore that she didn't know Solida was going to kill Bill. It had all happened so fast that she couldn't stop it. She said that Solida had threatened to kill her if she ever said anything to anyone.

At the subsequent trial George Solida was found guilty of murder and sentenced to 20 years. They also gave him a second sentence of 26 years for the charge of attempted solicitation to kill.

On June 15th, 1988 Lisa Pierce pleaded guilty to hindering apprehension and was sentenced to six years in prison.

22
POOR BARBARA

Barbara Mauger had been working at the sweet counter in a store in Philadelphia for only a week when he came in. He was a tall, good-looking man and he literally swept her off her feet.

Barbara was 17 and this was her first love. She took it very seriously. Soon she was inviting her beau home for dinner and to meet her parents.

The Mauger family were very impressed by him. He reeked of class. His clothes were neat and expensive-looking and his name alone was enough to bowl them over. He was called Russell St. Claire Bietzel and he worked at Blauners department store as the credit manager.

True, at 27 he was 10 years older than Barbara and he was also hard of hearing, occasionally having to cup his ear so that he could hear you. "But," as Barbara said after he left that night, "he's rich and he went to college and he speaks so many languages, even Chinese. He's fantastic. He lives in a little room at the YMCA and he teaches swimming there to the poor neighbourhood children."

After a week, and at Russell's urging, Barbara left her job and went to work at Blauners as a stenographer in his department. In no time at all Russell was in and out of the Mauger home, almost as though he were already a son-in-law and Mr and Mrs Mauger conceded that Barbara could not have done better if they had arranged the match themselves.

The Maugers began to plan a big church wedding and they were understandably disappointed three months later to discover that their daughter had eloped.

The news came in a letter postmarked Chicago and was penned in Barbara's own girlish hand. She and Russell, she wrote, were en route to Central America where he'd been made an offer to oversee the operation of a coffee plantation business. His presence was required immediately, and because it was so splendid an opportunity they had decided to leave at once, without farewells or anything, and be married on the way.

She would write again soon, she said, and when they had made their mark they would return to Philadelphia for the parental blessings. She knew they would understand.

The Maugers didn't quite understand; but as long as Barbara and Russell were happy...

The letter had hardly arrived when the scandal began to break. First came department store investigators with questions about the whereabouts of the missing pair. Russell Bietzel, they said, had absconded with some of the firm's money, at least $700. Then came the police with the news that the man who had lured away their daughter was already married, that he was the father of two sons.

The police left a little while later and the Maugers settled back uneasily and waited for a letter. A search meanwhile fanned out across the country and spread eventually to Central and South America and finally to Europe. Russell and Barbara were not reported anywhere. Day after day the Maugers waited. But no letter came, nor any news.

A little more than six months later, on August 2nd, 1928,

and a little more than 3,000 miles away – in Stone Canyon, just outside Los Angeles, California – two boy scouts who had been hiking in the woods stopped short when they saw a blonde woman's head peering up at them from under a bush.

They stared at the head. Then they turned and ran. They dashed to a cabin about half a mile away and told a man what they'd seen. He phoned the police.

When the detectives arrived on the scene they saw no blonde woman peering up from under a bush as reported by the scouts. What the two boys had seen was a human scalp with blonde hairs still adhering to it. The scalp clung to the base of the bush.

Two hundred feet farther down the mountain was the rest of the corpse. The mummified body lay on its back, nude, its right leg missing.

The detectives studied the body. It had been ravaged by wild animals. Its middle had been torn open from navel to pelvis. The internal organs had gone, and there appeared to be a tiny fracture on the left side of the forehead.

Unquestionably the woman had been young, probably no more than 20. The regularity of the features indicated she had been pretty. She had also been married. She wore a simple gold ring. The fingers were long and tapering, the nails gave evidence of careful tending. But the body itself was now little more than a shell, the skin burned brown by the sun and drawn tight about the bones.

On the bridge of the nose and below the left breast were two bullet holes. They were exit wounds. The woman had been shot in the back. A third bullet was later found, lodged in the spine. The coroner estimated that the woman had been dead from four to six weeks.

The detectives scoured the area, convinced that animals could not have got far with the missing leg in such dense underbrush. But they failed to find it. What they did find, hidden in the undergrowth a few feet from the body, was part of a baby's skull and two tiny leg bones.

The detectives returned their attention instinctively to the mummified body. They studied it carefully. They could see now from the pelvis that the woman had been pregnant.

The detectives worked through the remaining undergrowth, then climbed the 30 feet to the road above. Here, in the dust beside the verge, they spotted four shining objects: ivory-hued bone beads, and a length of broken thread holding them together. The discovery indicated the killing had probably taken place here. There had been a struggle, the woman had attempted to run away and had been shot in the back. The body had then been stripped and thrown over the side.

Identifying the corpse was not going to be easy. Detectives speculated that the girl's leg might have been removed because it had some sort of distinguishing mark. There was no identifiable characteristic on the rest of the corpse. Her ring, however, did provide a clue. It was stamped with a pawnbroker's code and traced to a pawnshop in downtown Los Angeles.

The pawnbroker remembered the transaction. It had taken place a couple of months earlier, on June 4th. "The girl couldn't have been a day over 18 and she was pregnant," he said. "The ring wasn't worth anything but I felt sorry for her." He had loaned her 50 cents on it. She had retrieved the ring four days later.

The broker opened his records and gave the detectives her address. She was Mrs Barber of 841 Golden Avenue, Los Angeles.

This address, however, turned out to be an apartment building and the manager said she didn't know any "Mrs Barber". But when detectives described the girl as blonde and pregnant the manager immediately declared that she knew who it was. "You must mean Barbara," she said. "Barbara Burholme."

Apparently the Burholmes had moved into an apartment in the building the previous April. Barbara was expecting her baby in late July or August. They seemed to be a fine couple, they paid the rent on time and gave no trouble. Originally, the manager thought, they had come from Pennsylvania, though they had also lived elsewhere in Los Angeles. They were not particularly unusual. Russell Burholme went off to work each morning. No one knew what he did, but apparently he had a good job and was well paid.

Barbara was plainly not happy, however. She often cried and there were times at night when she could be heard pleading with her husband. But what it was she pleaded about no one knew.

Then on June 24th, a Sunday morning, Russell Burholme rented a car and took Barbara out on a picnic, or so he said. When he returned that evening he was alone. "He told a ridiculous story," the manageress said, a story about how on their way home from the picnic they had gone by way of the ocean and that in Long Beach, his wife had spotted her aunt getting out of a cab at the railway station.

Barbara's aunt was returning to her home in the East, and on the spur of the moment Barbara had decided to go with her so she could be with her mother and father when she had the baby.

The following day Russell Burholme was seen burning many of his wife's things in the backyard incinerator. He even gave away Barbara's pet cat. A few days later, Burholme moved out himself. He had left no forwarding address and nothing had since been heard of him or of Barbara.

At police headquarters a wire was dispatched to Pennsylvania state police, describing the pair and requesting a check of local police and missing-person files. Eventually a dossier came back from Philadelphia. It gave all the known facts about Russell St. Claire Bietzel, alias Burholme. It also gave some details about Barbara Mauger, including the information that the girl's right foot was severely scarred.

Russell Bietzel was finally tracked down to an engineering company in Los Angeles where he had found work.

"You're police and you want to talk to me about my wife," he said as soon as he saw the detectives. "I'll tell you about it."

The detectives half expected to hear a confession. Instead, however, Bietzel told them of taking his wife for a ride in a hired car.

"We had a right old row," he said. "She was running around with another man. I guess she got angry. Anyway, she got out of the car and I never heard from her again."

"In her condition," said the detective sceptically, "expecting a baby in about a month, and she's running around with another guy!"

Russell Bietzel was arrested for the murder of Barbara Mauger. His trial began on September 24th, 1928. Evidence was put forward to show how he had driven his pregnant wife to the deserted spot. A taxi driver recalled driving Bietzel back to the place where evidently he had removed the leg from his wife's corpse, knowing this to be the only means of identifying her body. Her leg was never recovered, though a charred shoe buckle from one of Barbara's shoes was found in the back of Bietzel's garden.

It took only 40 minutes' deliberation for the jury to reach a decision. No one could be sure why he murdered Barbara Mauger. Was she just his play thing? Did his real wife suddenly turn up? Did the pregnancy scare him? No one knows. But Russell Bietzel was found guilty of murder in the first degree.

On August 2nd, 1929, exactly one year from the finding of Barbara's remains, Russell Bietzel dropped through the trap-doors at San Quentin Prison.

23
THE SNUFF KILLINGS

It didn't take a genius to suspect there was something wrong. He had offered her $200 just to find a couple of young hookers to be in his movie. But this was California, 1977. He could have got the girls themselves for half that amount. There were any number of young hookers who were only too willing to take their clothes off for a few bucks. Why, for the money he was offering she'd have agreed to do it herself. "So what's the joke?" she asked. Then the man gave her his story.

He told her he wanted to make a snuff movie. There was big money in it, he said. He could afford to pay over the odds. And if she wanted more money, she could have it. If, he said, "you could get the hookers and then kill them while I hold the camera, I'll give you $5,000 with more to come after the picture was sold."

At the time there was considerable publicity concerning a movie that was said to have come from South America in which young women were engaged in lesbian acts and then tortured to death. The victims were shown trussed to the rafters of a building and then slowly dismembered while the cameras recorded the torture. Its authenticity, and the authenticity of so-called snuff movies in general, had been much in question. Was it real or was it just good acting and clever camera tricks? As this madam looked at the man who was offering her this weird proposition she had a terrifying sense that she had just found out the answer.

With great presence of mind she told him she'd think about it. In fact, she would start right away trying to find the right girls for him. And then, without further ado, she said goodbye.

Immediately afterwards she went to the police. "Yes," she said, "he might just be crazy. But I've got a feeling he means it. I think he's done it before."

The police were sufficiently concerned with the woman's story to want to follow up the lead. As a consequence two female officers went undercover, to play the young hookers that the man had requested. Before they made contact with the would-be film-maker, however, investigators attempted to find out as much about him as they could.

His name turned out to be Frederick Berre Douglas. He was 49 years old and had a family. He had been married for 27 years and until recently worked as a furniture upholsterer. Now he was supposedly retired but they heard that he was in fact currently involved in the pornographic film business and apparently making good money from it ... They also learned that he was a self-proclaimed "reverend".

The two policewomen were instructed about the role they were to play. Each was equipped with small concealed weapons and tape recorders. They were told to get as much conversation as possible on the tape concerning what they were supposed to do and how much they were being paid for it. They were also warned to take care.

It was a typical hot southern California day when Fred Douglas picked up the two disguised policewomen and drove out to the desert. The temperature had passed 100 degrees when they reached the Yucca Valley. The officers who were following them in a convoy of unmarked cars were all sweating heavily.

Suddenly, Douglas's car turned off the main highway on to an isolated, flat area, dotted only by large boulders and a few trees. For fear of being noticed, the police convoy had to stay well back. It wasn't what they had hoped for. They managed to keep his car in sight, however, and watched as, several miles into the desert, Douglas pulled off the road altogether and stopped in front of an old wooden shack. The officers observed what was going on through binoculars and watched anxiously as their two colleagues were led inside.

The minutes ticked by as the anxious policemen kept their eyes on the building. Then one of them shouted: "They're coming out!"

Douglas emerged first, his hands clasped on the top of his head. The women officers followed, their guns drawn.

"He's all yours," they said."We've got what we needed on tape and he's been read his rights."

Some officers went inside the shack. They found a whole collection of instruments of torture. There were knives, bone saws, tourniquets, chains, ropes and leather straps. On a shelf were packages of what the officers described as "exotic female undergarments". There were also a number of books with titles like *Sexual Tendencies of Lesbians* and *Pain and Sexual Pleasure*.

A movie camera and a collection of still cameras, along with several rifles and pistols, were found in the boot of Douglas's car. But the officers found no exposed film, either in the shack or later at Douglas' home. Nor did they find any bodies.

For a week 60 men on horseback and in four-wheel drive vehicles, scoured the desert wasteland. Spotters in planes searched for possible grave-sites while men on foot probed with rods and metal-detectors. But they discovered nothing. Eventually they gave up. "We don't know if there are bodies out there or not," said a police spokesman. "The desert is a damn tricky place to find anything. There's a hell of a lot of sand out there and there's no way we're ever going to cover all of it."

Douglas was brought to trial, but it was almost impossible to make a case against him. He certainly couldn't be charged with murder, and even on charges of procurement it would be a hard battle. His defence could make a challenge on the grounds of entrapment. At the first trial the jurors simply could not agree on a verdict. They were dismissed and a new trial was ordered. In the event, however, no second trial took place. Instead, Douglas engaged in some confidential bargaining. He agreed to plead guilty to a much lesser charge and was granted probation.

The investigating officers were disappointed with the result, but at least it brought consolation. As one them said: "At least the crazy bastard won't try anything like that again."

Or would he?

Five years later, on March, 14th, 1983, a hiker in the desert near San Diego came upon two graves that had been disturbed by animals. The skeletal remains were brought in for examination and identified as being two white females, fairly young, possibly in their teens. The skull of one of the victims had been crushed but the cause of death for the second victim was undetermined, although crushed larynx bones indicated that she could have been strangled.

A search failed to reveal any clothes or other items that might help to identify the bodies. But when a check was made of missing girls in the area dental records revealed that the victims were Beth Jones, 19, and Margaret Krueger, aged just 16, who had disappeared some seven months earlier after meeting two men for a nude photographic session.

As a matter of routine the information was filed with the National Crime Information Center and a computer check returned the information on Fred Douglas and his alleged snuff movies.

Detectives ran a check and learned that Douglas and a man he worked with in an upholstery shop had hurriedly left the area shortly after the skeletons of the girls were found. Douglas was believed to have gone to Canada, while the second man, Tony Diaz, had gone to Mexico.

As the investigation proceeded, charges of suspicion of murder were filed against Douglas and Diaz and warrants were issued for their arrest.

Diaz was located in Laredo, Mexico, where, whilst awaiting extradition, he had made a full confession to Mexican police officials.

His statement detailed how he and Douglas had met the girls and offered them $500 to pose in the nude. Douglas had then forced them to commit lesbian acts, and also indulged in sex acts with them himself. Diaz then said that Douglas had cut the neck of the younger girl and drunk her blood before battering her head with a rifle butt. Douglas then strangled the other girl.

Fred Douglas was also located. He was picked up in Las Vegas, Nevada, having already fled from Canada when he had learnt that the police were on his trail. Unlike his partner, Douglas flatly denied knowing anything about the murders or ever having seen the girls. Asked why his friend had told the story he had, Douglas simply claimed that Diaz was a drug addict. He had probably dreamed the whole thing up.

The police thus had a problem, and it was a problem that grew even bigger when Diaz decided to withdraw his confession.

Everyone was certain that Diaz and Douglas were guilty, but they had no evidence to prove it. There were some circumstantial details, and a few witnesses would be able to prove the connection between the men and the two girls. But there was nothing much more, and it seemed unlikely that any substantial evidence would now turn up.

"Douglas tried to pull this same thing before and he got away with it," said the District Attorney, "and I don't want that to happen again. In my book, it's better to have one egg in the basket than the chance of spilling both of them out."

The detectives agreed. The only answer was to offer Diaz full immunity from prosecution in exchange for his testimony. The judge granted their petition.

There were gasps from the spectators in the court and the faces of many of the jurors turned white as Tony Diaz recalled how Douglas had cut the neck of pretty Margaret Krueger and then drunk her blood. Diaz told the whole sordid story. For three whole days he related the grisly details of how the victims had been lured to where they had been killed and the details of Douglas's sadistic practices.

On cross-examination Diaz was asked why, if he had not approved of Douglas killing the girls, he had not tried to stop him.

"I guess you could say that I'm a guy without much guts," Diaz responded. "I didn't know he planned to kill them when we took them there. But I didn't have the guts to stop him when he did. I was afraid of him."

The jurors deliberated for eight hours before finding Douglas guilty of the two murders. The seven-man, five-woman jury was then asked to deliberate a penalty.

In his plea that they should return with the death penalty, the prosecutor told the panel: "It's a horrible, heinous offence to snuff someone's life for your own selfish reasons. He mercilessly tortured and killed his victims, using their bodies to experiment with. Can anyone ask for sympathy and pity for somebody who has that sort of attitude towards his victims?"

The jury took only a few hours to return a verdict recommending that Douglas be sentenced to death.

24

A MONSTROUS COUPLE

"I don't march to the same drummer you do," declared Douglas Daniel Clark. "If we were all like me, Sodom and Gomorrah might look like a nice place to stay."

We may never know how many young women Douglas Clark murdered. Those who knew him said that his goal was to kill one hundred. He himself admitted to 50. In court the police claimed he had killed at least six, and a jury agreed.

The women Clark butchered were all creatures of Sunset Boulevard in Los Angeles: callow young runaways, brittle whores, black and white, all willing to spend a few minutes with him in the front seat of his car for the $30 or $40 they'd set as the price for their favours.

For the most part, all his victims died the same way. Clark paid them to have oral sex with him in his car, then shot them in the head with a small-calibre weapon when he reached his sexual climax. Next, he would strip off their underwear, saving it as a trophy. Then Clark would obtain his greatest satisfaction. He would copulate with his victim's corpse.

Gruesome and horrific as his practice was, however, what made Douglas's case even more horrid was the way he did not operate alone. In his ghoulish career during the summer of 1980 he was accompanied and assisted by a monster almost his equal. Clark's partner was a plump, middle-aged nurse by the name of Carol Bundy.

Clark and Bundy cruised Sunset Strip, looking for whores. Bundy wasn't too keen on the arrangement, but it was only because she was jealous. She complained about the way Clark liked to romp with skinny young streetwalkers and neglected her own charms. She would have preferred to have his attentions all to herself. Still, what she got she enjoyed. Bundy liked to boast about the way he made love to her. Clark, she said, was "talented" and "extremely good in bed." And Clark's penchant for killing did provide some thrills. "It's fun to kill someone," she said. They would often giggle about it when they were in bed together.

Clark's first known victims were 15-year-old Gina Marano and her step-sister Cynthia Chandler, aged 16. The girls had been missing for a while when, on June 6th, 1980, a friend of Cynthia's was called by someone who identified himself as "Detective Clark" and told her that the two girls were dead. The corpses of her friends were discovered soon afterwards. Cynthia and Gina had both been shot in the head and their bodies sexually abused.

"Doug Clark of Los Angeles police" called their friend again two weeks later, and described the manner in which the girls had been killed. "I killed them and now I want you too, " he told her. "I shot Gina in the head. Then I shot Cynthia in the heart, then I made love to them. Now I want to do it to you. I saw you at the party where they were." To add to the terror, the caller told the petrified girl he was having an orgasm while he was talking to her.

Before disposing of those first corpses Clark had attempted to find Carol Bundy and share his experience with her. That day, however, she was not at home. Clark left her a note – "sorry to have missed you" – and then drove the bodies away in his car to discard them like so much rubbish along a highway exit road.

On June 23rd, 1990, police found the bodies of two more young females. They were two young prostitutes, 20-year-old Exxie Wilson and Karen Jones, 24. Like Gina and Cynthia, these new victims had also been shot in the head with a small-calibre weapon, and they too had been sexually abused. But this time it was even more gruesome. Exxie Wilson had been beheaded, and her head wasn't anywhere nearby. Indeed, it wasn't found until three days later when a Burbank resident pulled into his driveway to find a wooden box obstructing his way to the garage. He got out of the car, opened the box and stared at the glazed eyes of the dead woman. The head had been frozen solid and wrapped in a pair of Levis. It was covered in garish make-up. It also appeared that the head and the hair had been washed in detergent.

This macabre twist in the killing was courtesy of Miss Bundy. The thirty-seven-year-old nurse had suggested that Clark should do something peculiar with his victims. "If you're going around killing hookers," she told him, "you might as well make it gruesome and do some weird things, like cutting the head off to make it look like some psychotic did it."

Bundy later said she was quite surprised when Clark took up her suggestion, and furthermore took it up with considerable enthusiasm. "When Clark first brought Exxie's head home he was laughing," she said. "He thought it was as funny as hell, that it would be a good trick to play on the cops – making it gruesome – make them think they'd got a real freak out there... I mean, he really didn't want to decapitate anybody. But the broad was dead anyway. What was the harm in it?"

Bundy first saw the head of Exxie Wilson when it was in the sink in their apartment. Clark had just taken it out of the refrigerator where he had frozen it solid. "I was essentially turned off by the head," she subsequently told detectives. "But we did have a lot of fun with it. I did her up to look nice, like a Barbie with make-up." Thereafter, according to Bundy, Clark would swing the head around by the hair and take it into the shower and orally copulate with it.

Another victim of the man now being called the Sunset Boulevard Killer was Marnette Comer, a 17-year-old runaway from Sacramento, California, who had last been seen on June 1st. A month later her mummified body was found by snake-hunters in a ravine near Sylmar, a community in the San Fernando Valley. Then the nude body of a teenage girl was found in the Saugus-Newhall area of Los Angeles County. She too had been shot in the head with a small-calibre weapon. The police concluded that one man was responsible for all six killings, and they feared that he would soon strike again.

Ironically, however, the next victim was not a woman but a man. Jack Murray was an old boyfriend of Carol Bundy. She had moved out from his apartment to live with Clark but the two were still in contact.

On August 9th, 1980, Jack Murray's body was found in his van, parked on a street in Van Nuys, only a few blocks from his home. He had been shot and stabbed numerous times and his head, which was never found, had been severed from his body.

Murray's van led the police to his home and a search there revealed his previous liaison with Carol Bundy. Bundy's new address was discovered and detectives went to visit her. They had already received information, probably from Murray himself, that she was implicated in the murders of the Sunset Boulevard Killer.

Bundy was taken into custody on August 10th and charged with the murder of her former boyfriend. Just 48 hours later, Clark was arrested and charged with the murders of the six young women. He was also charged with aiding and abetting Bundy in the murder and beheading of Jack Murray.

During questioning at police headquarters Clark, who said he had been wearing women's underwear since he was a kid, maintained he could never look at sex "head on" but that it had to be "kinky" to be any good for him. He said he had killed perhaps 50 women and was hoping to kill 100 in his pursuit of "kinky sex".

He said he sometimes saved the underwear of his victims and played with it. He also described his fantasy of cutting a girl's throat during intercourse, with his excitement increasing as she neared death.

According to Carol Bundy, Clark had hunted women on the streets at night like an animal, killing some of those he caught. His criterion, she said, for deciding whether a woman lived or died was her ability to successfully copulate with him orally. Failure meant death from a bullet in the head.

According to Bundy, she and Clark planned to kill increasing numbers of women and make each murder more gruesome than the last. She said that Clark would refer to such killings as "taking care of business". She said he kept a "killing bag" in his car, containing knife, rubber gloves and plastic bags.

In his conversations with the police, Clark said he preferred having a girl give him oral sex, then shoot her in the head when he reached a climax. He added that he had killed Marnette Comer by shooting her four times and then slicing open her abdomen to hasten the process of decomposition.

At his trial in the spring of 1983 Douglas Clark was asked if he felt any pangs of remorse for what he had done. Clark merely sneered. "If I had a violin, I would play it," he declared to the bewildered courtroom.

Clark remained bizarrely confident and cheerful through the proceedings. Even when the jury returned with the verdict of guilty on each of the six counts of murder he was still smiling.

On March 16th, 1983, Douglas Daniel Clark was sen-

tenced to die in the gas chamber. The sentence didn't
worry him. Indeed, the condemned man reacted to the
verdict with these words: "Within all due process of the
law, I want the execution within 10 days."

The judge went through the litany of pronouncing the
death sentence six times, once for each of the six sex-
related murders. The first time the death sentence was
mentioned Clark glared at the judge and grimaced. "Smile
when you say that!" he said. Then he said no more.

Two months later, as jury selection was about to begin
for the trial of Carol Bundy, she changed her plea of not
guilty by reason of insanity to guilty. She was later sentenced to life imprisonment.

25

PHOTOGRAPHED, RAPED AND MURDERED

Judy Ann Dull, Rose Arden and Lois Lee were three young models who shared a comfortable apartment in West Hollywood. All three made their livings posing for art photographers, and all were successful at their trade. Curvaceous, smiling Judy, however, was especially in demand for nude and scantily clad pin-up poses.

On the evening of Tuesday, July 30th, 1957, Judy and Rose were both out and Lois was at home, chatting with a friend who had come over for supper. At around 8 o'clock a slim, serious-looking man came to the door. He asked for Rose. The man introduced himself as John Glynn, a freelance photographer, and said that a friend had recommended Rose for a photographic assignment he had planned.

Lois told him that Rose was out for the evening but she allowed the photographer to come in and have a look through her friend's portfolio. She also showed him her own portfolio and Judy's as well.

"Now there's a girl I'd like to work with!" Glynn exclaimed when he saw the glamour shots of Judy. "She's just the type I have in mind. When can I speak to her?"

Lois gave him their telephone number and told him he would just have to try when he could. The photographer thanked Lois and assured her he'd be phoning soon.

John Glynn called Judy early on Thursday morning, August 1st. He explained that he had a rush assignment and wanted her to pose for him at 2 o'clock that afternoon. He had no studio at the moment, he said, but he would bring his equipment over to the apartment and they could do the shoot there. Though Judy had other jobs planned for the day, she agreed to see him.

When John arrived, Lois was at home with Judy. The young man explained that he had been able to get the use of a friend's studio and they ought to go there. He said the job would take a couple of hours and agreed to pay Judy her usual $20 an hour. He also wrote down the telephone number of the studio so she could be reached in case anyone should call for her.

Judy packed some things into her modelling case and at 2.15 p.m. they left the apartment together, John politely carrying her case for her.

The 19-year-old model was never seen again. The telephone number that Glynn had left was a machine shop on the other side of town, and evidently a number he had plucked out of thin air. There was no record of a John Glynn with any of the model or photographic agencies in the Hollywood area, and though the police talked with several dozen of Judy's friends, fellow-models and employers, not a single clue developed.

Three months later a ranch-hand found a body in a shallow, sandy grave in the desert country some 130 miles east of Los Angeles. Its dimensions and hair colour fitted those of Judy Ann Dull, but technicians estimated wrongly as it turned out that the corpse was of a woman aged between 30 and 35 who had been dead for six to twelve months. It seemed to rule out the missing model. The ravaged bones remained unidentified and the whereabouts of Judy Dull remained officially unknown.

Early in March 1958 a new disappearance hit the headlines. Shirley Bridgeford, an attractive 24-year-old brunette divorcee, mother of two small sons, had gone out on a blind date on March 8th and had not returned. The date had been arranged through a Friendship Club in Los Angeles who were subsequently contacted by the police. They gave the police the address of Mrs Bridgeford's date, but it turned out to be fictitious. They described the man as being about 25 to 35 years old, close to six feet tall, with light brown hair, blue eyes and a thick moustache. He had large protruding ears and wore glasses with light plastic rims. This description was similar to the one given to the police by Lois Lee, but nobody made the connection.

Three months later another attractive young woman went missing. The landlord of a small hotel in the Wilshire district of Los Angeles contacted the police to report the disappearance of one of his tenants. She was Ruth Rita Mercado, a 24-year-old dark-haired beauty of Latin extraction and a former strip dancer who, under the name of Angela Rojas, now earned her living as a glamour model. She went missing on July 23rd. Her clothes, jewellery and luggage were still in her room. So too was her beloved pet collie, who was almost dead from starvation when the landlord opened her door with his pass key. But of the woman herself there was no sign.

At 9 o'clock on the evening of Monday, October 28th, a man rang the doorbell of a modelling agency on Hollywood's Sunset Boulevard. The caller was a young man the manageress knew as Frank Johnson. He was an amateur photographer with whom she had worked before. Indeed, she herself had posed for him the previous summer before she had opened up the agency. Frank asked if she could come over to his apartment that evening and pose for some more shots.

The manageress felt uneasy about the request. She couldn't quite explain it but there was something about the photographer that made her feel uncomfortable. His taut, nervous face and those large, intense eyes set between his prominent jug ears made her nervous. Nevertheless, she agreed to his request. "OK," she said, "I'll come along if we can go in my car and take along a chaperone."

That didn't suit Johnson at all, however. He wanted to drive his own car and did not want any third person along. "I can't stand working with other people hanging around," he said. "Let's forget it. I'll find someone else."

The manageress then thought of Lorraine Vigil, a shapely, raven-haired 27-year-old who had arrived in Los Angeles a few months before. She was currently working as a typist but was determined to become a model. She had answered the agency's newspaper advertisements and was very eager for work. So far, however, they hadn't found her a single assignment.

The manageress picked up the phone and gave her a call. Lorraine was delighted. She told her to send him straight round. The manageress tried to warn Lorraine to be on her guard, and, after Johnson had left she called the girl back and made her warning more explicit. She didn't believe there was any real danger, she said. It was just a feeling she had that things weren't quite right.

Frank Johnson picked up Lorraine at about 9.30 p.m., blowing his horn and waiting outside in his black two-door coupé instead of coming to the door. As they started out Lorraine asked him for her $15 fee in advance. He handed her $10 and said he would give her the rest later. She then got into the car and they headed off to down-town Los Angeles.

"This isn't the way to the studio," remarked Lorraine after they had been driving for a short while.

Johnson looked at her. "We're not going to her place," he said. "She has some other people coming there. We're going to my own studio. It's down in Anaheim, but it won't take us long to get there."

Lorraine tried to make conversation. But Johnson said nothing, he just clung on to the wheel and continued driving. He increased his speed as they crossed the Orange County line and terror gripped the girl as they shot through Anaheim without slacking. The car sped on, leaving the city far behind.

It wasn't until they had reached Santa Ana, 35 miles south-east of Los Angeles, that the wild-eyed driver slowed down. He turned into a dark, lonely side road. Then the car stopped.

Lorraine guessed what was coming but she was too terrified to do anything. When Johnson pulled out a gun she thought her end had come.

"OK, kid," he said, "now I want you to do as I say. Do what I tell you and you won't get hurt."

Lorraine pleaded with him not to hurt her but this just made him angry. "If you don't shut up you'll really feel pain," he warned.

"All right, I'll do whatever you say," she stammered.

Johnson took out a short length of rope from his pocket, grabbed the terrified girl's left wrist and knotted the rope around it. He then tried to wrench her right hand behind her back, intending to tie her wrists together.

"Please don't tie me!" she pleaded. "I'll do anything you want if you just don't tie me."

"All right, but don't give me any trouble," her captor said, waving his gun a few inches from her breast. "Remember I can kill you any time I want."

Lorraine now lost all control. She started screaming and banging on the car door. Other cars passed, but none of the drivers noticed what was going on.

Johnson clapped his hand over her mouth and clamped his other arm around her neck. "People will think we're just necking," he laughed viciously. "I could choke you right now, if I wanted to."

Johnson now put the gun down and again tried to tie her hands. This time the wiry brunette tried to fight him off. Johnson reached for the gun again. "Right, that's it," he rasped. "I've lost all patience."

Frantic and knowing that her wild-eyed assailant meant what he said, Lorraine grabbed the muzzle of the gun and turned it away from her. They struggled furiously. Suddenly the gun went off. A bullet tore through the girl's skirt and burned her thigh.

Nearly out of her wits with terror and reacting out of sheer instinct, the little brunette seized this moment to reach around him with her free hand and open the car door on his side. She pushed it with all her strength and they both tumbled out on to the road.

Lorraine grabbed Johnson's gun hand and sank her teeth into his wrist. With a howl of pain, he dropped the weapon. Lorraine grabbed it. She scrambled to her feet and tried to pull the trigger. It didn't work. But she kept the gun trained on him and remained that way until the glare from a spotlight bathed the scene with light.

"What's going on here?" said a voice. It was Officer Thomas Mulligan of the California highway patrol.

Shortly afterwards Johnson and his intended victim were being escorted back to Anaheim and taken into custody. Later, tearful and shaken from her ordeal, Lorraine was driven home.

The jug-eared prisoner now identified himself as Harvey Morris Glatman, a 30-year-old television repairman. He readily admitted his attempted assault on the would-be model but he said he had done it on impulse and was sorry. He also acknowledged that he had already served prison time in New York and Colorado. He was then booked on suspicion of assault with a deadly weapon and attempted rape.

The next day Harvey Glatman filled in details of his past life and criminal history, which was confirmed by telegrams to police departments in other cities.

Born in New York City of respectable, hard-working parents, Glatman was raised in Denver, Colorado. He was arrested there in 1945, at the age of 17, for a series of robberies which also involved molestation of women and girl victims. He was sentenced to five years in the state prison for aggravated robbery. Released after less than a year, he went to Albany, New York, where he was soon in trouble again.

In August 1846 he was jailed as Albany's "phantom bandit", who had robbed and terrorised three women as they walked home from bus stops in lonely parts of the city. Armed with a toy pistol, he was arrested while stalking a fourth victim. He was convicted of first-degree grand larceny and sentenced to five to ten years. Paroled from Sing Sing in 1951, he was discharged from parole in 1956 and travelled West, finally landing in California by way of Denver.

Although Glatman talked readily about his long-past offences and his most recent attack on Lorraine, he was evasive about his activities in the Los Angeles area during the past year. After detectives had visited his home, however, they suspected that he had a great deal more to say.

Harvey Glatman's Los Angeles apartment was plastered with pin-up pictures of nude beauties, some showing the girls bound and gagged and in "torture" poses. They also found expensive photographic equipment and a collection of prints which Glatman had evidently taken himself. Some of these pictures showed an attractive blonde girl, bound and gagged and lying within the apartment. Others showed two women, similarly bound, spreadeagled on the desert sands. Subsequently these were shown to be images of Judy Ann Dull, Shirley Bridgeford and Angela Rojas, all of whom had been photographed in the agonizing few moments before their death.

"OK," he told detectives, "I killed those girls."

Glatman said he had never meant to harm his victims. He had only wanted sex from them. But then after he had raped them he was terrified of being caught. He killed them, he said, because there was no other option. "I truly hated to kill those girls, but it just had to be. Angela was the one I really liked and I tried to figure a way out for her. But I couldn't come up with any answer. So I finally got out the rope and did it, the same as I did with the others."

Throughout his two hours of recorded testimony, Glatman continued to claim that the only reason he had murdered these women was because he feared they would have him arrested for raping them. But it was clear that he had derived a twisted emotional satisfaction from each of his killings. In each case it had been the same method. Glatman had lured his victims out to a lonely place on the pretext of taking pictures. He raped them and then made them kneel down and tied their hands behind them with a short rope. "After that," he said, "I made them lie flat on their stomachs and tied their ankles together with one end of a long cord. I'd loop the middle part of the cord around their necks. Then I'd stand there and keep pulling on the other end till they stopped struggling. They didn't suffer much," he insisted. "Not one of them really knew I was going to murder her – at least not until the last few minutes."

At Glatman's trial the chief psychiatrist at San Diego, Dr Carl Lengyel told the court: "This man has always felt inferior to the opposite sex and could get real pleasure only in feeling dominant. He could feel so only in situations when the partner was helpless."

Convicted of murder on December 17th, 1958, Glatman was sentenced to die in the gas chamber in San Quentin prison. He displayed no emotion as he listened to the sentence and insisted that he wanted no appeals made on his behalf. "It was my own fault," he said. "I only want to die."

His wish was granted on September 8th, 1959, when Harvey Morris Glatman calmly entered the small greenwalled execution chamber. He sat quietly in the chair, awaiting the final action of the cyanide pellets.

26
THE CANNIBAL OF PARIS

Renée Hartevelt was a big, blonde, 25-year-old student of French literature. Dutch by birth, she had taken her first degree at the University of Leyden and was now engaged in post-graduate work in Paris at the Censier Institute.

Renée came from a wealthy family but, in Paris, she lived a very modest life. She occupied the maid's room in an apartment building at 59 Rue Bonaparte which she received rent-free in exchange for looking after the owner's two children at weekends. In addition she gave private lessons in French and German which provided her with all the funds she needed for her living expenses. It was an arrangement that seemed to be working extremely well.

On Saturday, June 13th, 1981, however, when she was supposed to be taking charge of the children, Renée was nowhere to be found. She was normally so reliable; it was not like her to go off without warning. Her landlord was concerned and, of course, more than a little daunted by the prospect of having to take care of his children himself. As the hours ticked by he finally decided to report her absence to the police.

At the police station Renée's landlord was given short shrift. A twenty-five-year-old, they told him, was old enough to do as she pleased. If she had decided to go off for the weekend, then that was her affair. If she was still missing on Monday, they said, he could visit them again and make an official report. Until then there was nothing that they could do. As a matter of routine they entered Renée's details into the police computer but the landlord was promptly sent on his way.

That evening, in a restaurant in the Bois de Boulogne, the huge park to the west of Paris, a number of diners watched in amusement as an oriental-looking dwarf with two enormous suitcases went hurrying past. It was a comical sight. The poor man had heaved the suitcases out of a dark blue 504 Peugeot taxi and was dragging them across the park on two little wheeled caddies. The suitcases were far larger and heavier than he was, and it made for a surreal spectacle.

Of course, it was a struggle for him, but the dwarf carried on regardless. Some 45 minutes later, however, he had apparently given up. He was no longer dragging them. Instead he was now trying to push them into the Bois de Boulogne lake. These efforts were witnessed by two girls who – rather daringly, perhaps – had chosen that evening to take a walk through the park.

The night was dark but the dwarf was clearly visible under the street lighting. When he heard the girls approach he threw them a startled glance and abandoned the suitcases where they lay. He then ran off into the bushes with amazing speed and agility – like a rabbit, as the girls later described it – and was gone.

Intrigued, the girls approached the suitcases to see what they might contain. They soon drew back, however. One of the cases was smeared with something that looked like blood. This was not the comedy they had expected. Petrified, the girls ran to the nearest public telephone to call the police.

Shortly afterwards an inspector arrived. Donning a pair of rubber gloves, he first ran a metal scanner over the cases just in case they might contain a bomb. Then, undoing the straps, he opened the first suitcase and peered in.

Inside he found a plastic rubbish bag that had been filled and tied. Using a sharp knife, he slit the bag and gingerly pulled it open. He peered inside. It was not a pretty sight. The bag contained a woman's face. Her nose had been cut off.

At the police morgue a pathologist made a more rigorous examination of the suitcases' contents. Between them the two suitcases contained the best part of a woman's entire body. Along with the head, the victim's torso and limbs had been cut up into convenient-sized portions and also packed in plastic sacks. The intestines and all the internal organs were present. The lips, one breast and large portions of the thighs and buttocks, however, were missing, as was the tip of the nose.

The manner in which the woman had been cut up seemed strange and ominous. Neither her hands nor her feet had been deliberately mutilated to prevent identification. The parts that had been cut away were all fleshy and soft, the sort of cuts that one might make in butchering an animal for meat. To add to the mystery the woman had been engaged in sexual intercourse either just prior to her death or shortly after it. There were traces of semen in the vagina.

In the suitcases the investigators also found what had apparently been the woman's clothing: a light summer dress, a brassière, white nylon knickers, short socks and shoes. Alas, there was no form of identification.

The pathologist eventually reported that the victim had been a large, blonde girl in her mid-20s. She had been dead for around 48 hours, and the cause of death had been a single .22-calibre rifle bullet, fired into her neck at the base of the skull at point-blank range.

As the process of investigation began, the police computer

came up with Renée Hartevelt. Her landlord was summoned to the morgue, as were a number of her friends from the university. They were only allowed to see the victim's head: there was a sheet covering up what remained of the body, so that they would not be aware that the head and body were not joined. The tip of the nose, which had been cut off, was replaced with wax to present as lifelike an appearance as possible. The identification was immediate and unhesitating. All those viewing the body agreed that this was Renée Hartevelt.

It didn't take long for the police to get further reports about the mysterious oriental dwarf and in due course they also managed to track down the taxi-driver who had driven him to the Bois de Boulogne.

The driver remembered his strange fare very well indeed. He said the dwarf had spoken very poor French and there had been a fearful struggle with the suitcases which were so heavy that it required his and his customer's combined efforts to get them into the boot of the car and out again. Asked where he had picked up his passenger, he said that it was in the Rue Erlanger. But he could not recall the number. Taken to the street in police car, however, he quickly identified the building. It was number 10.

A short time later detectives moved in and blocked off all the exits from the building. Then, to the amazement of onlookers, a detachment of plainclothes police, some in bulletproof vests carrying rifles, burst into the building and raced up the stairs.

Issei Sagawa was in his room. He was easily recognised and corresponded precisely to the descriptions that had been given of him. At 33 years of age he was a brilliant scholar with a Masters degree from the University of Osaka, where he had written his thesis on the subject of Shakespeare's *Macbeth*. He had been in France since April 1977, writing his doctoral paper on the influence of Japanese contemporary literature on French writing. His

French, however, was far from fluent.

Still, it was adequate enough for him to make a detailed confession of the murder of Renée Hartevelt and to describe the acts following it.

Sagawa's confession came readily. There would have been little point in denying the crime. The .22-calibre rifle was found standing in a case inside a cupboard and one of Renée Hartevelt's lips, her left breast, a part of her thigh and both her buttocks were found in the refrigerator. Asked by the appalled investigators what he had done with the rest of her, Sagawa calmly said that he had eaten it.

"Cooked?"

"No, sliced thin and raw," said Sagawa in his soft, gentle, slightly lisping voice.

He had met Renée Hartevelt, said Sagawa, at the university where they had been attending the same lectures. They were both interested in literature and had fallen into conversation together. A few weeks earlier, he said, he had asked Renée if he could come and visit her and she had agreed. On two occasions they had had tea in her room, where they talked about books and Renée gave him some help with his French.

Sagawa returned the invitation on Thursday, June 11th. He invited Renée for tea in his flat and she had cheerfully accepted. She thought of it as just another meeting to discuss literature. When she arrived, however, Sagawa asked her if she would like to have sex with him. "No, no," she replied, "we are good friends, but that is all."

Sagawa seemed to take her rejection in good heart. He didn't ask again. Instead the couple just drank their tea and resumed more normal conversation.

The two of them were kneeling on the floor, facing each other, when Sagawa got up and went over to his bookshelves to fetch a volume of poetry by Friedrich von Schiller. Giving it to Renée, he asked her to read one of the poems out loud. He then put a tape of suitably sombre music into the cassette recorder and as the music played and the girl read aloud from the book, he came up behind her and shot her with the rifle at the base of her skull. She died instantly.

Renée was now unable to resist his advances. Sagawa undressed her carefully, taking off all her clothes. Then, with her body still warm and pliable, he had intercourse with her.

Once he had reached orgasm, Sagawa pulled himself off the corpse and went to the kitchen. He came back with a razor and a knife with which he cut off the tip of Rene's nose and also a part of her breast. He ate these pieces of flesh immediately. Then, working slowly and methodically, he butchered the rest of the body, cutting off and storing in the refrigerator the parts which he proposed to consume later and dismembering what remained so as to be able to pack the parts into plastic bags. Every now and again he stopped his hacking and took a photograph of the girl's mutilated corpse. The undeveloped film of these gruesome pictures was also found in his flat.

Once his grisly work was completed, Sagawa said that he ate a little more of his victim's flesh and then went to bed. He slept soundly until late into the following morning. It was then that he packed the bags into the suitcases and made his arrangements to go to the Bois de Boulogne.

Arrested and taken to a detention centre for psychiatric observation, Sagawa expressed great concern that his act might result in bad publicity for his country and his people. He also declared his regret for the trouble that he had caused. But of remorse for the death of Renée Hartevelt he said not a word.

Psychiatrists called in to examine him began with the conviction that they understood Sagawa's problems very well. She was big, blonde, beautiful and white, they argued. He was small, dark and oriental. It was a question of his virility as a male and his pride as a Japanese that he wanted to conquer this big white girl. When she refused him he felt rejected and thus reacted with violence. All the rest was merely an attempt to dispose of the body.

Sagawa, however, would have none of this interpretation.

"No!" he declared. He had not felt particularly rejected, and although he found Renée sexually attractive, it had been more as a matter of novelty than anything else that the idea of having sex with her had occurred to him. After he had killed her he had sex with her corpse simply because it was available and there was no reason he could think of why he should not indulge himself.

The reason he had killed her was nothing to do with sex. He had killed Renée Hartevelt simply because he wanted to eat her flesh. Ever since his earliest youth, he said, he had dreamed of eating a young girl, and now that he had done so, he had found the experience every bit as satisfying as he had hoped.

At a court hearing on July 13th, 1982, Issei Sagawa was found incompetent to stand trial and was ordered to be confined for an indefinite period at the top-security section of the Villejuif mental hospital.

Sagawa, however, stayed in that hospital for only two years. In May 1984, following pleas from his wealthy family in Yokohama, he was transferred to a psychiatric institute in Japan. It was there that he wrote a book about his experience of eating Renée's flesh, "the most delicious meat I ever had".

In the Fog went on to become a best-seller in Japan, with critics raving about Sagawa's prose. One critic described it as "outstanding among recent Japanese literature". But, the book's success has not been repeated in other countries, for whilst the style may be superb, the content is horrific.

Sagawa's book begins with a long account of his growing infatuation with Renée Hartevelt. It has long, lingering descriptions of her "nice breasts, slender build, long white neck, transparent white skin, beautiful and gorgeous face..." It then goes on in gruesome detail about the author's experience of slicing her flesh and eating it and how he stored various parts of her body in his refrigerator so he would be able to savour them later.

In September 1985, after barely a year in the Japanese hospital, Sagawa was pronounced sane and allowed to leave. Not surprisingly, when news of his release reached France it caused outrage. In Japan too there are those who have grave doubts about the decision. Dr Tsuguo Kaneko, who treated Sagawa during his first months in the Japanese hospital, says the man is a psychopath and still potentially dangerous. He should be in a prison or an asylum.

The Japanese government, however, feel confident that Sagawa has been "cured". He is thus under no form of supervision or therapy and is an entirely free man. He is currently living in Japan, busily working on a sequel to his best-seller. He has also become something of a media personality.

27

HONEYMOON OF HORROR

Still drowsy after sleeping late on Sunday morning, December 1st, 1991, John Popovich watched as the sporty red Corvette screeched to a halt at the kerb in front of his house in Costa Mesa, California. An exotic young woman dressed in tight-fitting trousers, black gloves, a loose white blouse and dark glasses scrambled from the driver's seat and hurried towards him. She was trembling and crying. "I've been raped," she sobbed.

Omaima Nelson had visited John Popovich several times before. During the hot summer months she had been a regular guest at his barbecues and they had also seen each other at the local bars and nightclubs. That, however, was before Omaima's marriage, when the curvaceous 23-year-old had been happy and cheerful. Now things were very different.

"My husband's raped me and cut me," Omaima wept. "Please help."

Omaima then told Popovich a horrific story of how her husband had knocked her to the floor and then ordered her to strip. He had then tied her up on the bed and forced her to have sex. He pushed his penis into her mouth, she cried, demanding oral sex. Then he slashed her with a knife.

Omaima thought that some of her injuries might need first aid and began to show her cuts. She took off her gloves and displayed her bare hands, which were covered with scars and scrapes. Then Popovich watched in astonishment as Omaima lifted her blouse, pulled her right breast from the top of her bra, and revealed two parallel scratches, over two inches long, just above her nipple. Then she began to unbutton her tight black trousers to show even more.

"She pulled her pants down," Popovich would subsequently recall, "but I could already see the cut on her thigh. It was kind of visible through the vents on the side of her pants."

Despite her injuries, Omaima wasn't bad to look at. With her olive complexion, shoulder-length brown hair and voluptuous figure, she frequently caught the attention of men's wandering eyes. Her high cheekbones, wide mouth, full lips and smouldering brown eyes gave her an exotic sex appeal.

John Popovich knew some of her background, but not all of it. As a young child, Omaima Aref had lived in a squatter's section of Cairo known as the "city of the dead", so named because of its proximity to city's cemeteries. One of eight children, her early life had been far from easy. She was sexually abused when she was just a little girl and, at the tender age of six had been brutally circumcised.

Omaima was raped for the first time when she was ten. She was raped again in her teens. She never told anyone about it but she knew one day they would find out, and lived in fear of the consequences. A future husband's discovery of her violated purity could result in harsh punishment for her and dishonour for her whole family. She believed it might even lead to her being killed. Salvation arrived, however, when she was 19. It was then that Omaima met a young American who asked to marry her. She readily agreed. Love didn't come into it. She married him merely to escape her hopeless future in her native land. They moved to the United States in 1986.

The marriage soon foundered, and Omaima struggled with a series of unsatisfactory relationships before being divorced in 1990. She found work in Southern California, first as a nanny and then as a model.

In the autumn of 1991, in the Costa Mesa tavern she frequented to dance and listen to music, she met William Nelson, a brawny six-footer who at 56 was 33 years her senior. He was also an ex-convict. But he was still the best thing to have happened to her in a long while. "It was really nice," Omaima told her friends. "I was in love. I was looking for someone who was kind and nice and wouldn't beat up on me and would give me love... love I never found before."

Nelson took the beautiful young Egyptian to Phoenix, Arizona, and married her on the first day of November 1991. They spent their honeymoon driving cross-country, through Arkansas and Texas. But now, after four short weeks of marriage, something was terribly wrong.

John Popovich had been shocked by the sight of Omaima's injuries, and he tried to be sympathetic to her plight. As her story went on, however, he began to get worried. And then she said something that brought Popovich to the edge of panic.

"Can I trust you?" she said. "I need to trust you with my life."

Popovich asked what she meant. Omaima then made her confession.

"She told me that she had killed her husband," Popovich later divulged. "I asked her how, what happened? She said she was tied up on the bed while he was raping her and cutting her, but she broke loose with her right hand and reached over and grabbed the lamp and smashed her husband over the head with it."

Omaima said that when Nelson fell over unconscious she grabbed "the tool" he had used to cut her and stabbed him. She demonstrated it to Popovich with a wild slashing motion. "She said that she'd chopped him up in pieces and had cut off his head and she wanted me to dispose of it. She said that she had washed the blood off the body parts, wrapped them in newspaper, and put them in plastic bags and left them in the apartment. She wanted me to go over there and do some cleaning."

Omaima offered Popovich $75,000 and two motorcycles, he disclosed, if he would agree to help clean up the apartment and dispose of her husband's remains.

"She told me she took the head, hands, arms and legs, and other pieces to the bathroom to clean them up and wash off the blood in the bath. She washed the parts so they would be drained of blood so they wouldn't drip anywhere. She told me that when I disposed of the head I should make sure I crushed it, with the dentures, so there wouldn't be any trace of who it was."

Popovich didn't know what to do. But he agreed to help, hoping that this would stall her long enough for him to be able to call the police. But then there was a knock at the door.

Popovich told Omaima to remain calm and not worry as he cautiously opened the door and peered out. He was relieved to see only a friendly woman neighbour. Before letting her in he cautioned Omaima. "It will be better not to tell her what has happened," Popovich whispered. "She goes to church and she's a real peaceful person. I don't want to scare her. Let's just say that you got in a brawl with your old man over some girl."

Omaima heeded his advice and explained to the visitor that the cuts on her hands were a result of a domestic dispute. The kindly neighbour offered to clean, treat and bandage the wounds. Meanwhile Popovich told Omaima that he had to go out to the shops. The visiting neighbour offered to give him a lift, and Omaima agreed to wait in the house.

As soon as Popovich was clear of sight of his home he rushed to a public telephone. He called the Costa Mesa police.

At 2.05 p.m. Officer Danny Hogue arrived at Popovich's

house. A former member of the homicide squad, Hogue was an experienced interviewer, and Omaima, although startled at finding the police suddenly involved, was quickly put at ease. She answered his questions calmly.

Omaima told Hogue that her husband, Bill Nelson, was away on a business trip in Florida. She didn't know exactly where he was staying in Florida or when he would return.

Officer Hogue asked to examine Omaima's car and Omaima readily gave her permission. The car was in any case unlocked. The officer looked inside and found a plastic rubbish bag. He hauled it out and opened it. It contained bloody meat and internal organs. He couldn't tell if they were animal or human, but he had his suspicions. Those suspicions were confirmed when Hogue arrived at the upstairs apartment of William Nelson with a team of fellow-investigators. There was no answer to their knocks so they forced their way inside. Hogue noticed immediately that the inside front doorknob was bloodstained.

Full cardboard boxes near the entrance and tied plastic rubbish bags on the floor suggested that someone had packed to move out. In the bedroom Hogue saw an open linen basket at the foot of the bed that contained a blood-soaked sheet that was still wet. A large butcher's knife lay in the kitchen sink.

He opened the plastic bags and found human legs severed at the knee. Various other body parts were wrapped in newspaper and stuffed into another plastic bag. One contained male genitals. A woman detective removed a newspaper-wrapped bundle that was in a cardboard box and began to peel away the layers of paper. She recoiled in horror at the sight of a pair of severed hands, with the left ring finger hacked off. It would later be revealed that the hands had been cooked in oil, apparently to destroy the fingerprints.

A forensic scientist accompanying the detectives was curious about the neatly made bed, wondering where the bloodstained sheets had come from. He lifted the heavy mattress, turned it over and was appalled to find that the entire underside was drenched in blood. Obviously the body had been dismembered on the bed, then someone had removed the bloody sheets, turned over the soaking mattress, and carefully made up the bed. Several boots were strewn about the room. Each boot was covering a bloodstain.

Outside the apartment another detective sifted through the rubbish bin and found a pile of still-frozen, uncooked boxes of peas, corn, frozen dinners and other food, obviously removed from a freezer. He raced up the stairs to tell his colleagues. Slowly, in awful anticipation, they swung open the freezer door, An innocuous blue plastic tray, filled with foil-wrapped packages was all they saw. They lifted out the largest package and began to unwrap it. Hogue cringed as he peeled back the last layer.

Shrunken, sightless eyes gazed at him from a grinning skull. Some of the skin had been boiled away and the jaws were blackened from being partially cooked. The head had been scalped. The hairy flap of skin that had been sliced off was found in another package.

In a departure from normal procedure, the pathologist, Dr Ronald Katsuyama, was brought to the crime scene to begin an autopsy examination. He would later have the body parts taken to his lab, where he would spread the remains on a stainless steel table in a macabre reassembly for identification. The body parts proved to be all that was left of the missing William Nelson.

Meanwhile at the police station Omaima was being interviewed. In a well-lit room, seated in a comfortable upholstered chair, she faced her interrogators across a circular oak table. Haltingly, in a soft, trembling voice, she began a rambling story.

She repeated that her husband was out of town. With tears streaming down her face again, she said that her husband had raped her. She vaguely hinted that Nelson had also raped two other girls the previous March. The girls were missing, she thought, and their passports were in Bill's possession. This later proved to be a fiction.

Answering questions between sobs, Omaima said that Nelson had forced her to pose for "thousands" of risqué photographs. Denying any knowledge of the bags in the car, she said that she had given a man a lift to the launderette. Maybe he had left the bags in the car. She denied she had killed her husband. Instead she said she had received a telephone call. Someone had yelled into the phone: "Well, bitch, you got what you wanted!" the voice had said. "Look in the trash bag. Why don't you check in the kitchen? You want some hamburger?"

She had looked, Omaima said, and had seen the grisly remains. It was because of this that she had rushed over to Popovich's house for help. She thought maybe the bloody mess was someone her husband had killed.

"He's chopped up women before," Omaima claimed.

Before her trial Omaima Nelson talked at length to two different psychiatrists. During the course of her interviews Omaima's story changed in a number of ways. But essentially it remained the same. Her final testimony was that her husband was sexually assaulting her in their home on November 30th, 1991, when she reached for a pair of scissors, stabbed him, and then "freaked out". She followed up the stabbing by beating him with a steam iron until he was dead.

As she continued to tell her story, however, it became clear that her actions were far removed from any form of self-defence. And when Omaima began to relate how she mutilated her husband's dead body there was no one left in any doubt that, for all her prettiness and timidity, here was a fiendish monster of a human being.

Before Omaima started to mutilate Nelson's body, the psychiatrist said, she put on red lipstick, a red hat, and red high-heeled shoes. She explained that she was fascinated with the colour of her husband's blood and wore red to make her butchery into a kind of ritual. She worked at her savage task all night.

As she was cutting him up, the psychiatrists learned, she also began to devour her victim. Omaima Nelson admitted to the psychiatrist that she ate part of Bill Nelson's ribs after cooking them in barbecue sauce. One psychiatrist quoted Omaima's words: "I barbecued his ribs just like in a restaurant. I was sitting at the kitchen table and I remember saying to myself, 'It's so sweet, it's so delicious, I like him tender.'" Another recounted how she had hacked off Nelson's genitals, and stuffed them in his mouth along with his left ring finger. Omaima allegedly said she removed the finger because Nelson "always came home and instead of kissing me hello, he would take his finger and shove it in me... I hated that so much. It hurt and it hurt my feelings so much. Why couldn't he just be nice?"

At her trial all the psychiatric evidence pointed to the fact that Omaima Nelson was psychotic. One experienced psychiatrist declared that in his 20 years in practice he had never seen anything so bizarre.

The jury took six days to deliver their verdict. They found Omaima Nelson not guilty of first-degree murder. They decided there was insufficient evidence of premeditation. But they did convict her of murder in the second degree.

On March 12th, 1992, Judge Robert Fitzgerald sentenced Omaima Aref Nelson to the maximum possible prison term: 27 years to life.

Speaking after the trial, Detective Bob Phillips, one of the main investigators on the case, declared: "Omaima Nelson is the most bizarre and sick individual I've ever had the occasion to meet. No one needs to look to the Dahmers of Milwaukee or the Hannibal Lecters of the screen. A new predator has emerged named Omaima."

28

THE CHRISTMAS BOXES

Nina Housden looked down at the stupefied figure in the chair. In an almost casual movement, her right hand reached out to his lolling head and gave it a gentle push. He fell forward and the sound of his breathing changed slightly. But there was no other reaction. It was just as she had expected.

Three swift steps took her to the table, where she picked up the length of clothes-line cord. Three more steps brought her back behind the chair. One more glance at the windows assured her that the curtains were drawn then, feeling safe, she manipulated the cord into a large loop. Calmly, deliberately, Nina Housden slipped the loop over the head of her unconscious husband.

Nina's face betrayed no emotion as she grasped the ends of the cord and wrapped a couple of turns around each hand. She spread her feet slightly and took a deep breath. Then she pulled.

Charles Housden's head jerked upwards as the loop tightened under his chin. His chest seemed to expand in a reflex action, while his arms swung slightly. But there was no protest, no struggle for life. He was too far gone in his stupor. Nina held the tension in the cord until she was sure he was dead. Then she relaxed. She sat down on the sofa and lit a cigarette.

Everything thus far had gone exactly as planned, but

there was a lot still to be done. In a short while Nina was back on her feet and continuing with her work. First she gathered up the remnants of the little party she'd had with her husband – liquor bottles, glasses, empty cigarette packets and ashtrays – and took them to the kitchen. Then she returned to the living-room and did some dusting and tidying.

It took only a slight nudge to make Charles topple forward from the armchair to the floor, but she caught his shoulders and lowered them gently to prevent any noise. A little awkwardly, she grasped him under the arms and dragged his body into the bedroom, where with some difficulty she hoisted him on to the bed. Then she undressed him, item by item.

Next, Nina went through her apartment, collecting everything that had belonged to her husband, all those little things that he'd left the last time he had walked out on her. She put them in a shopping bag, together with the hat, overcoat and other clothing he had worn that night. Making sure she had the key to his apartment in her pocket, she picked up the bag and left.

Less than 15 minutes later Nina Housden was slipping into her late husband's flat in Highland Park, a Detroit suburb. In a short while all of Charles' belongings were placed where he normally would have put them: the hat on the shelf, the overcoat and suit jacket hanging in the wardrobe, the trousers draped over the back of a chair; shirt, tie and underwear tossed carelessly into a pile; miscellaneous other items dropped on the dresser.

"Let them figure that one out," she muttered, grinning to herself as she shut the door and hastened back to her own apartment. Nina was quite proud of this touch.

It was 4.15 in the morning when she got back to her own bedroom again. "You haven't moved a muscle, Charles," she said as she glanced at the naked figure of her dead husband on the bed. She chuckled at her joke.

Without further ado, Nina Housden undressed and

put on her nightdress. She walked over to the vacant side of the bed and was about to get under the covers when she changed her mind. Throwing back the blankets, she swung her husband's legs to the floor, then carefully lowered his upper body. She pushed the corpse under the bed. "Goodnight, dear," she said, chuckling once more before she climbed into bed and switched off the light. The time was 4.35 a.m. Nina was asleep in less than five minutes.

The following day, Tuesday, December 19th, 1944, the young murderess set about the most grisly part of her scheme. First she stripped to her panties and bra. Next, she retrieved from a corner of the closet a large cardboard box which had once held blankets. She brought it into the kitchen, then returned to the bedroom. Now she hauled Charles's body out from under the bed and dragged it to the middle of the kitchen floor.

From a drawer, Nina took two slender packages and unwrapped a meat cleaver and a carving knife. She tested the knife's blade with the tip of her thumb. "Sharp enough to slice hair," she murmured approvingly.

Soon she set about her grim task. It must have been a strange sight indeed as the shapely young woman, clothed only in her underwear, knelt on the floor and proceeded to dismember the nude body of her husband, neatly depositing each limb in the large box as she cut and chopped it from the torso.

It proved to be more difficult than she had anticipated, and as the hours ticked by fatigue forced her to pause more and more frequently. At each rest period she would push herself away from the carved-up cadaver, lean up against the wall, stretch her tired legs and light a cigarette. Finally, at about 10 o'clock that night, she was finished. But she had to spend another hour cleaning up the mess on the kitchen floor.

After that Nina ran a hot bath, dumped half a jar of bath salts in it, and luxuriated in the steamy scented water. At 11.20 she was in bed and asleep. Charles packaged parts lay on the floor beneath her.

When she woke the following day she had a quick breakfast and then set off to fill the car with petrol and oil and get some road maps before returning to the apartment. As soon as it became dark that night she would load the car with all her belongings and every last piece of Charles and leave Detroit for good. All she had to do in the meantime was to gift-wrap Charles. She'd been too exhausted last night to complete the job.

Nina hauled the result of her gruesome post-mortem surgery from its hiding-place under the bed and on to the kitchen table. She proceeded to put her dismembered husband in colourful Christmas boxes, wrap them in festive Yuletide paper, and tie each parcel with bright red ribbons and pretty bows. She loaded them into the back of her car, covering them with her own clothes, and drove off.

Nina drove very carefully when she left Detroit with her grisly cargo in the early hours of Thursday morning. At 10 o'clock on that chilly morning she had reached Toledo, Ohio. In no time at all, she thought, she would reach Paducah, Kentucky, her home town, on the outskirts of which, as she recalled from her childhood, there were numerous caves and gravel pits where Charles Housden's gift-wrapped body parts could safely be hidden.

The long hours of driving were taking their toll and she was extremely tired. But she didn't dare stop, vowing to carry on until she reached her destination. Suddenly, however, the matter was taken out of her hands. As she changed gears after pulling away from a traffic light, the engine emitted a series of weird, spluttering sounds, then stopped. The gauge showed plenty of petrol, but the car wouldn't start. There was nothing to do but call a garage and have the car towed in.

At the garage she got the bad news. "It's going to take two days to fix, lady," declared the mechanic. "You've got a hole in your crankcase and you've lost all your oil.

The motor is all but burned out."

"Two days?" Nina echoed dully. Her heart sank at the thought of the parcels on the back seat, but what could she do?

"All right," she said finally. "Get it done as soon as you can. But I'll stay in the car while you're working."

The mechanic looked at her incredulously, but he couldn't talk her out of it. She got in the front seat and sat there determinedly as the men began work on her car. At midnight a new shift came on duty and took over the work, stealing furtive glances at the good-looking girl who insisted on staying in her car. When the shift changed again at 8 o'clock Nina sent a boy out for wine and sandwiches. She ate in the car, then sipped wine from the bottle.

By Friday afternoon the heat in the garage began to take its inevitable toll. Unpleasant smells started to emanate from the back seat of the car. One of the mechanics commented to Nina: "Lady, I don't know what you got in that back seat, but it's sure smelling up the place."

Nina had been bracing herself for this. "Oh, that?" she chuckled. "That's just some venison. I got a deer up in Michigan last week."

"You'd better do something about it soon," remarked the mechanic. "It's spoiling on you."

Nina laughed. "Shucks, no," she said. "Venison has to age, everybody knows that. The older it gets, the better it tastes."

The mechanic walked away shaking his head. Nina continued to sip from her bottle of wine.

The hours passed and the mechanics continued to work. Eventually, however, the combination of alcohol and fatigue caught up with Nina Housden. Her head lolled back on the seat and she fell asleep. Even the pounding noise from the adjacent car body repair department did not disturb her slumber.

Several hours later, Nina was still sleeping and the

obnoxious odour from the back of her car had become almost unbearable. Finally, one of the mechanics banged on the driver's door beside Nina to see how soundly she was sleeping. She never stirred. Then, easing open a rear door, he pushed Nina's clothing aside until he saw the gaily-wrapped Christmas packages.

As the clothing was removed the stench became even stronger. He lifted one of the packages and carried it to the workbench, where his co-workers clustered around him as he carefully unwrapped the "gift". As he lifted off the lid, they all gasped. In the box was a man's leg.

Nina Housden awoke a little later to find a man shaking her.

"Wh-what do you want? What's the matter?" she asked sleepily.

"I'm Detective Captain Ralph Murphy, Homicide Squad," the man said. "You'd better come with me."

It was one a.m. on Christmas Eve before Nina finished telling her macabre story. She was later returned to Detroit, where she repeated it again. Nina was calm, unemotional and in complete control of herself. Her tone was quiet, almost casual. With her soft Southern accent, she seemed no more excited than she might have been in recounting the details of an uneventful shopping trip. Her voice broke momentarily, only once: "Charles wasn't really such a bad sort of fellow. It's just that he ran around with other women."

Four months later, at her trial, she was found guilty of murder in the first degree. On May 8th, 1945, Nina Housden was sentenced to life imprisonment and taken to the Detroit House of Correction.

29
EDWARD GEIN: PSYCHO

Augusta Gein never left any doubts in her young son's mind that women were creatures of evil. On stormy nights in their gloomy farmhouse outside Plainfield, Wisconsin, she would open her heavy Bible and read him the story of Noah. Mother and son then prayed together for a second flood to wipe out the scarlet sins of modern women. Women were worthless, she warned him. Worse, they were also dangerous: they would plot against his virtue. They were to be avoided at all costs.

Ed and his elder brother, Henry, were discouraged from marrying or even dallying with the female sex. Instead she kept them busy working on the farm. Ed was a middle-aged man when his mother suffered her first stroke in 1944 and in all probability he was still a virgin. Shortly afterwards Henry died, trapped while fighting a forest fire. When Mrs Gein had a second stroke a year later, and died as a result, Edward Gein was left all alone, isolated, inexperienced and decidedly peculiar.

It was then that he sealed off his mother's bedroom and other parts of the house and set up his quarters in the remaining bedroom, kitchen and shed. He stopped working on the farm, too. A government soil-conservation programme offered him a subsidy, which he augmented with work as a local handyman.

With free time on his hands for perhaps the first time in his life, Ed Gein began to develop an interest in anatomy, female anatomy in particular. He got dozens of books and periodicals on the subject and spent hours poring over them. "After my mother died in 1945," he later declared, "I developed an uncontrollable desire to see a woman's body."

Soon the diagrams and pictures in his books were no longer adequate. He wanted to see the bodies in the flesh. This is not an unusual desire for a man, of course, but the method which Gein used was far from normal. Gein began digging up female corpses from the Plainfield Cemetery, the same cemetery in which his mother was buried.

Armed with a shovel and jemmy, he would disinter the corpses and drag them back to a shed behind the farmhouse and store them. Later he would dissect the bodies and spend hours familiarising himself with their anatomical structures. Sometimes Gein would also remove certain parts from the corpses in their graves, carefully covering up the traces of his work when he had finished. He would keep heads, sex organs, livers, hearts and skin. Gein's collection of macabre trophies grew and grew. So too did the range of his experimentation and obsession.

No one saw him at his work. No one ever suspected it was going on. In all Plainfield's population of 680 there was not a single mind twisted enough to imagine what unholy acts Edward Gein was performing.

It was in the winter of 1954 that Gein made the switch from digging up corpses to manufacturing them. His first victim was fifty-two-year-old Mary Hogan, the owner of the Pine Grove Tavern. She disappeared shortly after midnight on December 9th, after bidding her last customers goodbye. She was never seen alive again.

Whether Edward Gein killed any other women in the succeeding years is open to doubt. Certainly there are

those who have their suspicions. But it was not until
three years later that we are certain he struck once more.
His victim was Bernice Worden, the owner of a hard-
ware store in Plainfield which she ran with the help of
her son, Frank, a deputy sheriff. On the night of Friday,
November 15th, 1957, Ed Gein came over to the store,
bought some ice-cream and ordered a quantity of anti-
freeze. He said he'd pick up the anti-freeze the following
day and asked Frank if he would be at the store. He said
he wouldn't. Saturday was the start of the deer-hunting
season. "I'm going out to get the biggest buck in the
country," said Frank. "Mom's going to mind the store."

On Saturday morning the sun was obscured by clouds
and the day was decidedly grey. The Plainfield streets
were almost deserted. The men, with their guns, had
long since departed for the woods.

Bernice Worden was alone in the store when Gein
walked in. He handed her a glass jar which he needed to
be filled with anti-freeze. As she filled it and began to
write out a sales slip, Gein walked over to the gun rack.
He took down a hunting rifle, slipped a cartridge into the
breech and shot the woman in the head. She died instantly. Gein then locked the door to the store, dragged
Mrs Worden's corpse out of the back door and took it to
his farmhouse. He also took the store's cash register.

Frank Worden returned home at about 5 p.m. and
was surprised to find the store locked and dark. He entered the shop and found his mother missing and a pool
of blood on the floor. He also saw that the cash register
had gone. A sales slip for anti-freeze, half completed by
his mother, was on the counter. Worden remembered
that Gein was planning to stop by the store in the morning, and when he later spoke to Sheriff Art Schley he
said that Ed Gein was probably behind his mother's
disappearance. It was decided that Gein should be found
and arrested. He was picked up at a grocery store on the
other side of town.

There are conflicting accounts about what followed. So horrific were the subsequent discoveries that even the most official accounts seem to have become confused. Some have Captain Schoephoerster breaking into the Gein farmhouse. Others tell of Bernice Worden's son, Deputy Sheriff Frank Worden, being the first police officer to get to the Gein home. The most commonly accepted version, however, is that Sheriff Art Schley and Frank Worden arrived at the house together.

They parked their car in front of the Geins' bleak farmhouse and Schley pounded on the front door. There was no answer, so they walked around to the kitchen. The kitchen door was locked, but another door, leading to the summer kitchen, was ajar. The summer kitchen was a jerry-built one-room addition to the house.

Schley pushed the door wide open, entered and took a flashlight from his pocket. He flicked its switch and, for a single instant, his heart stood still. In a thick voice, he called out: "Frank, don't come in here! Stay outside."

But it was too late. Worden had already entered the room. He stood beside the sheriff. In the most horrible moment of his life, he saw what had become of his mother.

Bernice Worden's body was hanging upside-down from a beam in the ceiling. Steel meat-hooks had been thrust through the sinews of her ankles. She was stark naked and her head was missing. Her stomach had been slit open and she had been eviscerated like a deer.

Frank Worden uttered a wild, anguished cry. He ran out into the night and threw himself down on the ground. The sheriff managed to retain some self-control and continued to cast the beam of his flashlight around the room. A moment later he found Bernice's head. It stood grimly on a shelf and had been wrapped in cellophane. The skull had been sawn away just above the eyebrows. The head had been hollowed out and was stuffed with old newspapers. Schley's flashlight beam hovered on other grisly items in the room, but the sheriff had no desire to investigate much further. Instead he called for back-up.

Early on Sunday morning Gein's farmhouse, which was a virtual pigsty, was crawling with police officers. Technicians from a mobile laboratory based in Madison, the state capital, were called in and a generator was installed to power the arc-lights that would now illuminate the chamber of horrors they found inside the kitchen and elsewhere. It was worse than any of the officers had ever imagined.

In all ten human skulls lay about the summer kitchen. In the regular kitchen was a cardboard box containing an assortment of human noses. On a pan on the stove lay a human heart in some water. They found the complete front skin of a woman, including breasts. This had a cord to suspend it round the neck. Gein later confessed that he would wear this gruesome garment on moonlit nights and prance about the yard. There was also a shoe box containing nine vulvas, one of which appeared to be relatively fresh.

The laboratory men found four chairs in the dining room which they said had been upholstered with human skin. They also came upon a home-made tom-tom, consisting of a half-gallon can, the top and bottom of which had been covered with tautly stretched human skin. The investigators also found a waste-paper basket, a lampshade, a bracelet and the sheath of a hunting knife, all of which had been fashioned out of human skin.

Gein had also found a way to make genuine shrunken heads by peeling off the face and scalp of his victims and stuffing them with newspaper. He had nine of them, all with their hair, ears, lips and noses all intact. Some had been treated with oil to keep them supple, others showed traces of lipstick. And one of those shrunken heads was recognised as being that of Mary Hogan, the woman who had vanished three years before.

While these grim discoveries were being made Ed Gein

was being questioned at length at the Waushara County jail. He was then taken to the crime laboratory and from there to Dane County Jail. Extensive interrogations took place at each of these locations.

Gein did not deny anything, though significantly he admitted to the killings only when he was not being recorded. But his speech was vague and hesitant. An extract from one of these interrogations gives some idea of what transpired. Gein is talking to Allan Wilimovsky, one of the forensic experts.

"You told me that you removed some sections of the flesh," said Wilimovsky.

"Yes," replied Gein.

"What section of the flesh did you remove?"

"The head."

"The head? How about the vagina?"

"Well that – not always."

"In removing the head, did you first cut through and then snap the bone?"

"I guess that would be snapping."

"Would you work the head back and forth in the same fashion as you would when you try to break a piece of wire in two?"

"That's a good description of it. I never took any saw to the cemetery."

Wilimovsky then asked some searching questions about Gein's inner thoughts on sex.

"Did you ever have the thought that you would have liked to remove or cut off your penis and preferred to have it the shape of the sexual organs of a woman?"

"Well, part of that is true."

"What part is true?"

"That like removing part of myself."

"Does that part mean your penis?"

"Well, it does seem like it. But it seems like that was before, when I was young."

"Do you ever have any recollection, Eddie, of taking any of those female parts, the vagina specifically, and holding it over your penis to cover the penis?"

"I believe that's true."

"You recall doing that with the vaginas of the bodies of the other women?"

"That I believe I do remember, that's right."

"Was there a resemblance in some of these faces to that of your mother?"

"I believe there was some."

"How about the face? Have you ever placed the faces over your own face?"

"That I did. I'm pretty sure of that. The parts sort of like eyes, those parts of a head. There should be some parts of just a head and I suppose there would be about two or three."

"Well, do you remember how you held the faces over your own face?"

"I believe there was a cord."

"Do you think you would wear the face over a prolonged time?"

"Not too long. I have other things to do. Maybe an hour or so."

"Would you ever put a pair of women's panties over your body and then put some of these vaginas over your penis?"

"That could be."

Later, when he was asked why he killed Bernice Worden and why he cut her up, Gein gave the following explanation:

"Well," he said patiently, like a psychiatrist explaining a difficult point to an obtuse layman, "you see, it was sort of a sex problem. I blame all my trouble on my mother. She should have made me a girl.

"I almost never went out with girls. I was afraid of them. All I could think of was my mother and how much I really loved her. At one time, I wondered if some sort of operation could change me into a woman. I used to read a lot in books about anatomy.

"After my mother died I began to visit cemeteries at night when the moon was full. I had heard from an aunt of mine who worked in a lunatic asylum that patients went wild at this time of the month. One night I dug up the body of a woman who had just been buried. I took it home. It gave me a great deal of satisfaction.

"Then I began to watch the papers for obituaries of women. The night after they were buried, I would go to the cemetery and open their graves. I would cut the bodies up at home. I kept the skin and certain other parts and burnt the rest in my stove. I liked the women's hair. I used to put oil on the faces and other parts of the bodies, to keep them from drying out."

"I made masks from some of the faces. I used to wear them around the house. From the torso of one woman, I made a skin vest. I used to wear that too, along with certain other parts. I felt that if I wore a woman's face and other things of her anatomy, it might make me more like the woman I really wanted to be."

Ed Gein now sighed heavily. "I wonder if I could have a cup of coffee?" he asked.

Edward Gein was committed for life to an institution for the criminally insane. He died on Thursday, July 26th, 1984, at the ripe old age of 77.

The Gein home was burned to the ground on March 20th, 1958.

The film *Psycho*, based on the novel by Robert Bloch, directed by Alfred Hitchcock and generally regarded as one of the finest film thrillers ever made, was based on the Gein story.

30
THE FAMILY KILLER

Robin Martin's illness was a puzzle. He was suffering
from diarrhoea, vomiting and terrible stomach pains.
These are the classic symptoms of stomach ulcers. But it
is not usual for a fellow of 26 to get stomach ulcers.
Doctors at the Veteran's Hospital in Biloxi therefore
looked for another cause, and they found it. Robin Martin had been poisoned. He had been systematically fed a
diet of arsenic. Over the past two or three months he
had ingested an almost fatal dose.

It was clear that the poisoner had to be someone close
to him. His wife was the obvious suspect.

Ronald and Rhonda Martin had been married for four
years. They had wed in Pratville on December 7th, 1951,
and now lived in a small flat in Mobile, Alabama. They
were an odd couple. Rhonda Belle Martin was nearly 20
years older than her husband and what charms she may
have had had long since faded. She was neither beautiful
nor glamorous. One would have thought it more likely
that she was Ronald's mother than his wife.

And, extraordinarily enough, that was exactly what
she was. Or, more precisely, she was Ronald's stepmother.
She had married his father, Claude Martin, three years
previously. Claude, however, had died shortly afterwards.
It was then that she married his son.

Police investigating Ronald's poisoning were naturally

intrigued by this unusual state of affairs, not least because it was illegal under state law. They wondered also how Ronald's father had met his death. They were not too surprised by what they found but they still cringed as they listened to Claude's doctor tell them about his patient's last days. Claude's fatal illness had been accompanied by diarrhoea, vomiting and excruciating stomach pains.

It was time to investigate Mrs Martin's background a little more closely. Police soon discovered that Claude had not been her first husband. She had previously been married to one George Wetlaw Garrett. They had married on May 2nd, 1928. He was also dead. Pneumonia was the supposed cause.

George Garrett wasn't the only unfortunate member of Rhonda's family. As officials delved into the birth and death records of the Garrett family they were appalled by what they found. It seemed that being a Garrett was in itself a mortal disease.

Five of the Garrett children had died, and though their death certificates mentioned various illnesses as the cause of death, when the doctors who treated them were questioned it was discovered that acute diarrhoea, vomiting and stomach pains had been present in every case.

It was learned, too, that Mrs Mary Frances Gibbons, Rhonda's mother, had died in 1944 and that she too had suffered the same symptoms and agonies in her last illness.

There was now no doubt in the minds of the investigators that they were dealing with a mass poisoner who, undetected, had committed a series of fiendish crimes over a period of 20 years.

The exhumation of Claude Martin's body was set for March 2nd. An examination of his internal organs, his hair and his fingernails revealed exactly what the police had expected. Even now, five years after his death, his body contained an appreciable amount of arsenic, enough to kill several men.

As detectives awaited the full details of the toxicologist's report they made other discoveries. Claude Martin's life had been insured for $4,500; so too had George Garrett's. Each of the Garrett children had also been covered by a small life insurance policy. And Ronald was also covered by a policy valued at $3,000.

Rhonda Martin was arrested on March 4th, 1956. She showed no signs of surprise or fear and remained perfectly calm as the charge was explained to her.

"I don't know why you're doing this," she remarked as the officials escorted her to a car. "There's nothing to it at all. It's just a lot of nonsense."

"Ronald will be heartbroken when he finds out what has happened to me," she declared, "I love him so much. We've been so happy together."

Detectives made a thorough search of the Martins' apartment. They looked through a lot of boxes and medicine containers, but could find no arsenic. They did find a Bible, however. Rhonda had methodically inscribed in it a record of the frequent births, marriages and deaths in her family circle. And there were plenty of deaths.

In the meantime the authorities announced that they intended to exhume the bodies of George Garrett, Rhonda's mother, Mrs Gibbons, and the five Garrett children. Rhonda seemed unconcerned. She continued to deny that she was a poisoner, although she did talk a great deal about her background.

She disclosed that there was still another husband in her life, a man she had married when she was 15. This marriage had ended in divorce four years later.

The authorities went ahead with their exhumation plans. They began by disinterring the remains of George Garrett and one of Rhonda's daughters, Ellyn Elizabeth. Further exhumations were abandoned when, on Monday night, March 12th, 1956, Rhonda Martin finally confessed.

In a written statement many pages long, she admitted

that she had fed arsenic to Claude Martin, George Garrett, Mrs Mary Frances Gibbons and three of the Garret children: Emogene, Ann Carolyn and Ellyn Elizabeth. She had bought it, she said, as ant poison. Rhonda Martin insisted that no ant poison had been given to her two other daughters. They had died of natural causes.

The poisoning of Claude Martin was done at the dinner table. Rhonda had put two spoonfuls of the poison in his coffee at each meal for three months.

George Garrett's demise was accomplished in a much shorter time when she poisoned his whisky for several days. Finally, when he came home sick from work, she dispatched him with one last poison and whisky cocktail.

The murder of three-year-old Emogene was, she said, a spur-of-the-moment decision. The child asked for a drink of water because she couldn't reach the tap. Peeved, Rhonda dosed a glass of milk with the deadly powder and gave it to the girl. Ann Carolyn, too, died from a single glass of poisoned milk. Ellyn Elizabeth, Rhonda's 11-year-old child, suffered the most. After drinking poisoned milk for a year, she lost the use of her limbs. Rhonda, after watching the child's crippled condition "for a spell," gave her a lethal dose and finally ended her torment.

As an afterthought, Rhonda Martin also confessed to the attempted murder of Ronald, the one whose illness started the whole enquiry.

Rhonda Belle Martin's trial began on June 4th, 1956 and lasted only an hour. A jury found her guilty and sentenced her to die in the electric chair. She was put to death on October 11th, 1957.

31
WICKED WIFE'S
SIX ATTEMPTS AT MURDER

For 45-year-old Noeleen Hendley it all began when her son became engaged to the daughter of Terry McIntosh, a widower. Terry lived at Little Eaton, a few miles from the Coniston Crescent home of Noeleen, on the Breadsall Estate on the outskirts of Derby, and as soon as she saw him she knew he was the man of her dreams.

They met, as parents do, to discuss the arrangements for the forthcoming marriage of their children, but it wasn't long before wedding preparations were the last thing on their minds. Even before the ceremony was booked Noeleen and Terry were making passionate love at every opportunity. "We had sex as often as possible," Noeleen would later say. "I had never experienced such sexual practices before. I couldn't get enough of him. The days never seemed long enough. Terry was like a sex drug. He just took me over completely."

As their romance continued Terry McIntosh began to urge Noeleen to leave her husband and come and live with him. But she refused. Divorce, even separation, she claimed, was against her Catholic faith. The couple therefore continued their liaison in secret. And in this they were remarkably successful. Noeleen's son and Terry's daughter knew that their in-laws were getting on well together. But they never suspected it was anything more than that. As for Noeleen's husband, Tony, the poor man didn't have a clue what was going on.

It was McIntosh who first suggested that life would be easier if Tony Hendley were to die. The idea was little more than a joke to begin with, but then it took root. Neither of the two lovers thought they were capable of doing the killing themselves, but maybe they could hire someone to do the work for them. Discreet questions were asked as to how such a killer could be found.

Paul Buxton was not a professional hit-man. But the 41-year-old engineer was accustomed to violence, and was quick to see that there was a quick profit to be made out of helping Hendley and McIntosh with their plan. He agreed to do the killing, for a price, and a deal was sorted out. Noeleen would give him a £1,000 down-payment and a further £1,000 when the job was done. A further two or three thousand pounds would be paid when everything was settled.

The trio then set to work on a plan.

At first it was little less than a fiasco. Five different plots were hatched to get rid of the unwanted husband, and for a variety of reasons – mostly because Buxton lost his nerve at the last minute – each one of them failed. But then, on the evening of November 1st, 1991, the sixth plot was put in action.

It was shortly before the Hendleys' silver wedding anniversary. Terry McIntosh took the hapless husband to the pub for a drink. It was an outing designed to get him well and truly drunk and to allow time for Noeleen to set the scene at the house. Tony Hendley thought that Terry was just being friendly and, from the amount of drink he laid before him, generous as well.

Back at home Noeleen Hendley peered out of her kitchen window, anxious to see that no nosey neighbours were looking out. Then she opened the patio doors and let Paul Buxton in. He too had taken precautions, wearing a balaclava helmet and gloves to prevent identification.

As soon as he was in the house he dashed up the stairs and hid, holding in his hand the rolling pin with which he meant to batter his victim.

Tony arrived home exactly on cue. A little the worse for drink, just as he should have been, he went upstairs to use the toilet. Paul Buxton was ready. As soon as his victim's back was turned, he struck. Twenty-nine blows rained down on the man's skull.

Noeleen Hendley hurried upstairs to be greeted by the awful result of this brutality. Her husband's face was a "blob", as she later told police.

She went back downstairs and handed Buxton the first cash instalment before he punched her in the face as part of the scene-setting to make the attack look like the work of a burglar disturbed in the act. Then Noeleen let Buxton out by the back door.

Noeleen gave the hitman enough time to make his escape, then she ruffled her hair and ran out into the street. She screamed hysterically, crying for help. A short while later she and her fatally injured husband were in an ambulance and screeching towards the hospital. But for Tony Hendley it was too late. He died two days later.

For three months Noeleen grieved publicly, wearing black at all times, weeping at the graveside and even appearing on television to appeal for public help to catch the killer. She went to Mass three times on a Sunday and spent her spare time serving hot soup to homeless and down-and-outs. But at every opportunity she was still having sex with the man who had helped arrange the murder.

Detectives worked patiently on the case. A crucial pointer came from Noeleen Hendley's son. While visiting his new father-in-law he found a saucy photograph of his mother which Noeleen had given her lover as a memento of their steamy sex sessions together. He agonized for weeks over what to do, then he finally went to the police.

Before long the investigators had unravelled the whole

case. All three conspirators were arrested, and all of them made their confessions.

The murder trial of Noeleen Hendley, Terry McIntosh and Paul Buxton began in Nottingham Crown Court on November 18th, 1992. They were found guilty.

Mr Justice Holland sentenced the trio to life imprisonment, telling them: "This case has been distinguished by wickedness which will live long in my memory".

He described Hendley as a woman "besotted with her lover and consumed with hatred for her husband as a result." He went on: "It was not just the fundamental wickedness of plotting to murder a man, but the fact that it was persisted with over a period of a month. It culminated in a murderous attack, the brutality of which, I suspect, surprised even you."

After hearing herself sentenced the ice-cold Noeleen Hendley collapsed in the dock and had to be helped down to the cells by prison warders. Scuffles broke out in the public gallery between members of the father's family and the guilty wife's relations. Meanwhile other onlookers applauded the verdicts and the sentences.

32

HE HAMMERED HIS
DAUGHTER TO DEATH

Derek Fleming was the 51-year-old manager of a join-
ery company in Yorkshire. Slight and grey-haired, he
lived in a comfortable semi-detached house in Greystone
Avenue, Elland, near Halifax. He drove a company car,
earned a good salary and enjoyed a happy family life. In
short, Derek Fleming was a contented man.

But all was not as it seemegd. Though married for the
best part of three decades and utterly devoted to his two
children, there was a worm eating away at the centre of
his cosy world. He had a secret lover. Fleming had been
cheating on his wife for a long time. For the past sixteen
years he had been seeing another woman, even taking
her on secret holidays. Mrs Fleming apparently suspected
nothing.

In 1993 Fleming's affair was coming to its conclusion.
He had always promised he would marry his mistress
when his children had grown up, and now, with his 21-
year-old son away in Greece and Linda, his 23-year-old
daughter, talking of marriage, that time was drawing near.

On Wednesday, January 20th, 1993, Fleming and his 45-
year-old lover were in a pub poring over brochures for
apartments in Spain. They had finally decided to go ahead
with their plan. That summer the two of them would
leave England, fly to Spain and be with each other for

ever. Fleming would break the news to his family at the end of March.

So what happened between Derek Fleming and his daughter the following day? Could it have been that she found out about his plan and chose to confront him? Did she see those brochures in the pocket of his coat? Or was it as Fleming later claimed merely an argument about him spending too much time at work?

Mrs Fleming was surprised to find her husband at home when she came back for the shops that Thursday morning but he said he had felt unwell and had returned from work just a few moments before. His wife noticed that he had changed his jumper and trousers. A neighbour idly pointed out that the utility room appeared to have been recently cleaned. But these things weren't important at the time. They only became significant later.

Linda was nowhere to be seen. But, of course, she should have been at work. Yet she wasn't at home in the evening either. Mrs Fleming assumed that her daughter must be staying with a friend. But then she didn't come back the next day and Mrs Fleming began to get very worried.

Her husband telephoned Linda's boyfriend and asked him if she was there. Her boyfriend hadn't seen her. Mrs Fleming was now frantic and decided to contact the police.

Normally the police would not have taken a routine missing-person report particularly seriously, but they had an uncomfortable feeling about this one. There seemed to be no reason why Linda should have left home. Her disappearance was inexplicable, and the police feared foul play from the start.

An investigation began immediately but it didn't seem to get anywhere. They still had no idea where Linda was. A week later the police arranged a press conference in the hope of jogging someone's memory. The conference was televised, and looking straight into the camera, with his wife on one side and Linda's boyfriend on the other, Fleming made his tearful appeal: "We all love you," he said. "We want you home with us. Wherever you are, please come home or give us a ring."

Even this did no good. But it couldn't really have been expected to. Fleming's plea was a farce. He knew that Linda would never call and he knew exactly where she was. Her body was lying in the moorland ditch where he had dumped her after battering her over the head with a builder's hammer.

On January 31st Linda's corpse was discovered by a couple walking on the moors at Scammonden, above Halifax. Examining the body, a pathologist found severe head injuries, with deep lacerations. Linda's skull had been fractured in several places. She had been struck nine times, and there were also signs that an attempt had been made to strangle her.

Now, with a murder to deal with, the police redoubled their efforts to trace Linda Fleming's last movements. But they already had their suspicions about what had happened. They had noted discrepancies in Fleming's account of himself. They had also found out about his mistress.

Forensic experts conducted a thorough search of the house in Greystone Avenue. On grouting between the tiles in the utility room they discovered traces of human blood, and on a peg-bag in that room they found even heavier bloodstaining. They concluded that Linda had probably been killed in her home.

How had her body been taken to the moors? An examination of Fleming's car provided the answer. On the underside of the boot were more traces of Linda's blood.

"I don't believe what I'm hearing!" shouted the angry father as he was charged with his daughter's killing. But as the damning scientific evidence was put in front of him he broke down and confessed.

He said he had had a blazing row with Linda on Thursday morning and she had shouted at him and pushed him. Fleming claimed: "At that moment I felt extreme anger, possibly for the first time in my life." He said he grabbed her. "I was pushing her backwards, swinging with the hammer, I remember it connecting with something, just where or what I cannot say. Linda went down on the floor. I saw blood."

Fleming maintained that it had never been his intention to deceive the police, claiming that he had blotted the incident from his mind because it was "so awful, such a mess..." He said that after dumping Linda's body he had completely forgotten about it. "It was as if when I closed the boot of the car nothing had happened."

The trial of Derek Fleming began at Leeds Crown Court on January 17th, 1994. He pleaded not guilty to murder, but admitted his daughter's manslaughter.

On January 25th, Fleming's 52nd birthday, the jury took less than four hours to reject his plea and find him guilty of his Linda's murder. Fleming stood impassively in the dock as the verdict was given and the sentence of life imprisonment passed.

It was never established why Derek Fleming had turned on his daughter. But Detective Superintendent Michael Saunders, who led the investigation, has no doubts. "I think Linda suspected for some time about her father's double life. On that day she was going to have it out with him. I cannot think of any other reason for the killing."

33

I KNOW WHO KILLED
MUMMY AND DADDY

The wind was whistling outside the Greens' home on
the evening of January 4th, 1930. It was a beastly night.
Three miles away from the nearest town of Laden, Utah,
James and Lola felt even more isolated than usual. But at
least they had a full house. Normally they just shared
their small farmhouse with James's grandmother, Hannah,
and their young daughter Lois. But tonight they had two
other guests. Gladys Green and her baby girl had arrived
for a visit.

Gladys was Lola's daughter by a former marriage. But
she was also related to James. Gladys' husband, Delbert,
was James Green's nephew. It was a confusing kinship,
but one that probably wouldn't last much longer. Gladys
and Delbert were not well suited. They argued continuously. Divorce was only a matter of time.

It was quite a squash that night as everyone tried to find
somewhere to sleep. The farmhouse had only two bedrooms and one of those was downstairs. It took some
time to sort it out. In the end it was decided that Lois
and her grandmother would sleep in the bedroom upstairs and Lola, Gladys and her baby would sleep in the
second bedroom. James would have to make do with the
couch in the kitchen.

By 11 o'clock everyone was asleep except for James

Green, who was lying awake in the darkness. Suddenly there was a knock on the door. James got up, slipped on his overalls and went to see who it was.

"What do you want?" he asked the black figure outlined against the windy darkness.

The intruder made no reply, but simply stepped past the big farmer, waving a dimly burning light about him. Its rays fell across the door to where Gladys and Lola were sleeping.

Slowly, he moved towards them and, alarmed for the safety of his loved ones, James tried to push past and stop him. The man shrugged and then whirled round. A gun blazed out in the darkness. James Green staggered back as the bullet struck. In agonized pain, he clutched at the wound and fled out into the night, pursued by the gunman.

"For God's sake don't shoot me again!" pleaded the stricken man, lurching towards the gate at the roadside. The killer paid no attention to his cries. Another shot echoed in the night sky.

Terror gripped Lola and Gladys as the madman returned to the house and waved the gun in their faces. He didn't say a word as his finger pressed on the trigger again and again. The women fell.

Hannah Green, awaked by the bedlam of screams and shots downstairs, shook her granddaughter.

"Lois, wake up and run for your life! Run to Uncle Dave and tell him to send help."

The child sprang from her bed, and without donning a coat or even shoes fled from the room and dashed downstairs. Then she saw the bodies.

"Mama, are you hurt bad?" she sobbed, running over to her mother's side and grabbing at her.

"Yes, darling, she is," said Lola softly. "But you must go. Run, darling, run,"

Lola then turned towards the gunman.

"Don't shoot her! Please don't shoot my baby!" she implored, as the little girl, clothed only in her white nightgown, turned and ran away from the house of horror and to the safety of her uncle's home.

As she was running Lois heard two more shots ring out from the farmhouse. Those shots had been for her grandmother, she felt sure. But she dared not stop. She ran even faster.

News of the massacre quickly spread through the small community of Layton. It horrified everyone, and the police knew they would have to act fast. Even whilst little Lois was still dazed they tried to find out what had happened. Thankfully the little girl had been mistaken in thinking that those last shots had been for her grandmother. Though very shaken, the old woman was unhurt and was able to speak.

"Mrs Green, I wish you would tell me what you know of tonight," said Detective Bostic.

"I don't know much," the old woman replied. "We were all in bed and I was awakened by a shot. Jim screamed, then Lola and Gladys. They were all dead, all but the baby. It was like a nightmare."

"Have you any idea who did it?" the detective persisted. Mrs Green sobbed and shook her head.

"I know who did it. I saw him."

Lois's little voice startled everyone in the room and all eyes turned on her.

"You saw him?"

"Yes," she said with a voice that had now dropped to a faint whisper. The child looked around nervously. "It was Delbert," she said.

"Are you sure, Lois?" asked Sheriff Mann.

"Well, I think it was. I couldn't see very well and he didn't say anything but it looked like him."

Delbert Green was arrested that same afternoon. He insisted he knew nothing about the killings and had had nothing to do with them. He said he had been at home the entire time and had a witness who could back his story up. It was difficult to doubt him, but the man's calm attitude to the ghastly killings made the detectives feel certain that Delbert Green was the culprit. He didn't even ask if his baby had survived the murderous attack.

Green persisted with his claim of innocence until detectives retrieved his coat which was damp, as though it had been worn out in the snow not many hours before, and felt through its pockets. There they found a .32 Smith & Wesson pearl-handled revolver. It had recently been fired.

"Delbert, isn't this the gun you used to shoot James Green?" asked Detective Bostic.

The man's reply shocked the seasoned investigator.

"I don't know," he said calmly, "I sold the gun I used to shoot him with."

Delbert then began to talk.

"I killed them," he said. "I don't know why I killed Uncle Jim, because we were always good friends. But when I went in the house we went in the bedroom to talk to Gladys and Aunt Lola started to yell. I said something and Uncle Jim grabbed me. So I shot him first.

"Ever since Gladys and I were married, we've been bickering. Yesterday I told Gladys that if she thought she could do better she should try it somewhere else without me. I had told her that before, but we always made up. So I thought we would last night but when I came home, she was gone. She left a note to say she was going home.

"I went over to my mother's for a while. Then I left and went home and to bed. I couldn't sleep, so got up and went downtown and bought that gun. I don't know whether it is the one I used to have or not, but I bought it last night at a second-hand store, then drove out to Layton."

"If you knew she had gone, why did you go down there?" the detective asked.

"I went down there to either make peace with that family, or have peace for ever," he said. "I told Uncle

Jim I wanted to know what Gladys wanted done with our things. He said he didn't want to be mixed up in our affairs and to go and talk to her.

"I went into the bedroom and asked her what she was going to do. She said she was staying right there. It was then that Uncle Jim grabbed my arm and I turned and shot him. Aunt Lola and Gladys screamed, so I shot them too. I didn't want to let them suffer, so I shot them twice, once before Lois came running in and once after she left. I didn't try to hurt her, nor Grandmother. I then left and drove back home and went to bed."

Two days later, after a coroner's jury indicted him for the triple slaying, a charge of murder in the first degree was filed against Delbert Green. The charge listed explicitly the murder of his uncle, James Green. The two other charges were held in abeyance. He was arraigned the same day and came to trial on the morning of March 3rd, 1930, two months after his crime.

At first Green claimed insanity, but the testimony of two psychiatrists, summoned as witnesses for the state, blocked the plea. On March 6th Delbert Green was found guilty of murder in the first degree and made an appeal for a new trial. The appeal was denied and on May 17th, 1930, he was sentenced to die.

This execution, however, did not go ahead because a further appeal to the state supreme court suspended the sentence until the higher court had rendered its verdict.

To the amazement of everyone, the supreme court did grant a new trial and the whole process had to begin again. Finally, however, it came to an end and in March, 1932, Delbert Green was again convicted of murder in the first degree and again sentenced to be executed.

But the case was not yet closed. Now a second appeal, requesting a third trial, was filed before Utah's supreme court. However, this was denied and the conviction in the lower court was upheld. Delbert Green was remanded for re-sentencing. This time the killer was sentenced to be shot at sunrise on June 26th, 1935, at the state prison.

His fate now seemed to be sealed. But Delbert Green continued to persist with his appeals. Late on the evening before the execution was to take place, Governor Henry H. Blood granted the triple slayer a reprieve. The case lingered on under consideration for six months until finally Governor Blood, apparently deciding that a term of life imprisonment was inadequate for such a vicious crime, reaffirmed the sentence of death.

On January 23rd, 1936, Delbert Green was, for the fourth time, sentenced to die before a firing squad. On Friday, July 10th, 1936, the sentence which had been postponed for more than four years was finally carried out.

34

THE LODGER, THE LANDLADY AND HER DAUGHTER

Albert Goozee moved into the Leakeys' home in
Alexandra Road, Poole, Dorset in the summer of 1955.
England was then enjoying something of heat-wave and
the house was stifling. Nowhere was it hotter than in
Goozee's bedroom, which had no windows. He went to
bed with his door open. No one, he thought, would
disturb him.

Two weeks after he arrived, however, someone did
come in. She walked across the floor and sat down on
the side of his bed. It was his landlady and she was
crying.

"Oh, Albert," she sobbed. "You don't know how miserable I've been!"

"Why, what's wrong, Mrs Leakey?"

"My husband treats me like a beast. We haven't slept
together for years. Oh, please, hold me in your arms for
just a minute."

She slipped into bed beside him.

Albert William Goozee was a healthy 32-year-old. His
landlady, Lydia Margaretta Leakey, was a woman well
past 50. Her husband, Tom, was snoring steadily in the
back bedroom. Her thirteen-year-old daughter, Norma,
was asleep in the front room. Albert knew what he had
to do.

"You'd better go back," he whispered as kindly as he could. But it was too late. Even as the words came out of his mouth Mrs Leakey had slipped off her nightgown and was pressing her warm flesh against his. And the worst was still to come.

As Albert turned to embrace his landlady's softness in his arms a figure suddenly appeared in the open doorway. It was Norma!

"Mum, are you in here?" she called.

"Norma! Go back to bed," her mother rebuked.

"Mum, I'm ashamed of you. I'm going to tell papa," the child retorted.

"Oh, Norma," pleaded her mother. "If only you were grown up you could understand how miserable I've been."

"I am grown up, and I do understand," said the child.

Albert didn't doubt it. Norma still wore the concealing dresses of a grammar school girl, but underneath was the mature body of a woman.

"Then for God's sake, Norma, forgive your wretched mother and go back to bed."

"No, I can't sleep alone. I'm going to tell papa, unless..."

"Unless what?"

"Unless you let me get into bed with you. I'll go right to sleep, I promise."

"Heaven help us!" cried Mrs Leakey, but she had no choice but to comply. "All right," she said, "get in."

Albert had already moved to the edge of the bed and Mrs Leakey squeezed up close to him. Norma climbed in.

My God, thought Albert. The landlady, and now the landlady's daughter! Where will it end?

Five or ten minutes passed. Norma was breathing rhythmically, and if she was not asleep she was making a good pretence of it.

"She's asleep," whispered Mrs Leakey.

She turned to him again, and her warm body drew itself to him. Albert had sworn to himself that he would do nothing while Norma was there, but he hesitated. In another moment, his private promises were forgotten. But then, just as he was beginning to return her caresses in earnest, he saw that Norma's eyes were watching.

"She's not asleep!" he whispered in alarm.

"Oh, God! but I can't help it," said Mrs Leakey, almost crying. "I don't care! I don't care about anything!"

At breakfast, Norma seemed extremely pleased with herself. "I want some new records, some rock'n'roll," she said.

"I'll buy you some today, luvvy," said her mother, ladling Albert another helping of porridge.

That night the same thing happened. Mrs Leakey joined Albert in bed. This time, however, there was less fuss about Norma. It now seemed accepted that she would be there in the double bed. By Sunday it had gone even further.

Albert, Lydia and Norma were enjoying a pleasant afternoon picnic, eating sandwiches and drinking wine, when Lydia began to caress her lodger.

"I can't wait till tonight," she giggled, ruffling Albert's hair.

"Neither can I," chimed in Norma.

"Why, luvvy?" asked her mother.

"Because Albert's going to make love to me, too."

Albert sat up with a start. "Don't be ridiculous," he shouted.

"Norma, for shame," said Mrs Leakey, "Besides, you're only thirteen."

"That's old enough. I read about a girl who got married when she was twelve."

Did she really mean it, Albert thought. Or was this more of her blackmail?

There she sat, the little devil, but he had no intention of having sexual relations with her, no matter what. A girl of thirteen was jail-bait.

"It's the wine, luvvy," said her mother. "The wine and your foolish mother. You'll forget all about it when I buy you those rock'n'roll records."

Albert had a hunch it would not end there and he decided it would be best if he moved out of the house pretty quickly. But two more weeks slipped by and Norma said no more. This, however, was not to last.

A few nights later, Albert heard someone creep into his room and he looked up. It was Norma. She rushed to the bed and threw her arms around him: "Albert, I can't stand it any longer. Please, please!"

"Get out of here before I spank your bottom until you can't sit for a week," he warned.

"I'll scream and wake up papa!"

That quietened the lodger. Tom Leakey might be frail and weak-willed, but if he thought that Albert was trying to rape his 13-year-old daughter, who knows what he might do. He might even have a gun.

"Damn it, you little blackmailer," hissed Goozee. "What can I get you to make you go back to bed?"

"A wristwatch," she said.

"All right, Norma, I'll buy you a wristwatch." With that he watched the girl skip out of his room.

Albert needed no more encounters of that sort. The situation had become intolerable and drastic action was called for. It would have to come to an end. Albert Goozee had toyed with the idea of joining the Army for years and now he resolved to do just that. It would at least get him away from that little vixen. He signed up the next day.

Alas, however, this proved to be a terrible mistake. Albert didn't like soldiering. He had hoped to be stationed in England where he could meet a nice girl and perhaps get married. But the Army sent him to Cyprus where, being at the height of the war for independence, he was liable to be shot at any moment. Within a few months he was desperate.

Mrs Leakey came to the rescue. She put up the money

to buy him out, and as a consequence, in next to no time, Albert Goozee was back in Dorset.

It was all much the same in Alexandra Road, but if anything had changed, it was Norma. She had now turned 14 and visibly ripened. Albert was also pleased to find she made no new demands. She didn't even mention the promised wristwatch. He bought her a box of chocolates and a record now and then, and she seemed content.

But was she merely biding her time? Did she have some sort of pact with her mother? Subsequent events seemed to show that she was.

By now Norma was sharing the bed with Albert and her mother about every other night and one evening, as all three lay together, Lydia made her announcement: "Albert, I am no doubt a very foolish woman, but I have been thinking. When I was Norma's age, I wanted to make love more than anything. But I didn't. Then I married Tom and he was a clumsy idiot. I was sorry I had waited. So..."

Albert wondered what she was getting at.

"Go on, Mum," Norma urged.

"So, if I would act differently if I had my life to live over again, why should I deny my daughter what I would do if I were her age again?"

"My God," Albert thought, "she wants me to have intercourse with her daughter. And she is going to be in the bed with us. I've got to get out of this."

Albert knew he had to leave, but confronted with the charms of the ripening Norma, it was a difficult decision for him to make. Indeed, he remained at the house for nearly a month before he eventually made up his mind. But then, over the breakfast table, he finally told them. He said he just had to move away before something really tragic happened.

He was surprised how well Lydia and Norma took the news. They didn't even ask him to stay a while longer. It wasn't until he returned home that evening that he suddenly realised why. There, standing at the kerb was a shiny new car.

"It's yours," said Mrs Leakey, "I bought it with my own money, just as I bought you out of the Army."

Albert had never had a car before. He couldn't resist it. Lydia Leakey was smiling happily, and she and Norma were holding hands.

"So we are all made up," Mrs Leakey concluded. "You stay here and be happy with us."

Albert continued to stay with the Leakeys. He even drove them out for picnics every Sunday afternoon. Albert was happy and life was sweet. Sweet, that is, until the inevitable happened.

"Goozee! You are having relations with my wife!"

It was Tom Leakey, standing in Albert's doorway, shaking with anger and fear.

To Albert this was almost a relief. He'd known it had to come some time, and he was glad that Tom had said wife and not daughter.

"Now look, Tom," Albert reasoned, "I've simply made it right between you and your wife, that's all. You don't sleep with her, so I've done it for you."

"That's not the lodger's business!" yelled Mr Leakey. He raised a trembling fist and Albert gave him a push. Mr Leakey fell back on to a table and then to the floor.

"Get out of this house, Goozee! Get out, or I'll call the police."

Albert Goozee turned tail and fled. After months of dithering, he knew that he now had to go. He left the Leakeys' home and found lodgings elsewhere. It was, he thought, all over. A week later, however, he received a letter. It was from Lydia and her daughter, pleading with him to come "back home". Mrs Leakey said she would make no more demands on him. She would be happy just doing his washing, cooking and ironing. Albert was not persuaded. He ignored the letter. But they wrote again. This time they begged for "just one more picnic," and to this Albert relented. As a result, on Sunday, June 17th, 1956, Albert, Lydia and Norma set out in the car for Bignell Wood near Cadham, in the New Forest.

Could it end this easily? Albert was sure it would not. But it had to finish, even if he had to go to the police himself. That morning he began a letter to the Chief Constable of Bournemouth: "This is to state to the police that I have had to worry for a long time about Mrs Leakey. When I first went to her house, after the first two weeks we had intercourse. The young daughter was in bed with us at the time..." He intended to show this letter to Mrs Leakey to frighten her off.

At the picnic he chopped wood with an axe to make a fire. They had forgotten a bread knife, so he used an eight-inch stiletto knife instead.

Goozee's version of the events which followed were later taken in a statement.

"Norma," said Mrs Leakey. "Please go and see if you can find some bluebells."

Norma slipped off and Mrs Leakey turned to Albert: "Can't we get together again? Or go away together?"

"What about Norma?"

"We could take her with us."

"It's better if we end it now."

"Oh, no, no! I can't bear it."

She began crying and threw her arms around him. He tried to push her away but she clung on.

"I won't let you go! I won't let you go!" she cried.

Then Albert saw Norma standing over them. She had the axe in her hand.

"Why don't you leave Albert alone?" she screamed.

"No! I won't! I'll never let Albert go."

Albert saw the axe coming down. It hit Mrs Leakey just behind the right ear. Blood gushed as she struggled to her feet and staggered away.

Norma was screaming insanely. All Albert knew was that he had to stop that screaming. He hit her on the jaw, all his weeks of indecision and frustration going into the blow. He felt the bone crack, and Norma collapsed.

The next thing he knew, Mrs Leakey was standing in front of him. She had the stiletto in her hand.

"This is the best way for it to end. I'd rather be dead," she said.

According to Albert he thought she was going to kill herself and he lunged for the knife. But he missed and felt it go into his stomach. The eight-inch blade was half buried in him. He felt dizzy.

"What have I done?" moaned Mrs Leakey.

Albert thought he was dying. He jerked the knife out of himself and plunged it into Mrs Leakey.

Norma was behind him.

"What have you done to my mother? Why don't you do the same to me?"

Albert was blacking out. He didn't remember "doing the same to her" but the knife went into her chest and heart. Albert slid to the ground.

He came to an hour later. Mrs Leakey was lying on her back. Norma was lying on her right side, her head on her mother's outstretched hand. They were both dead. Goozee covered Mrs Leakey with a blanket and Norma with a coat. Then he got into the car and drove down the road. When he saw another car coming he got out, holding his stomach.

"There's been a murder in the forest," he said, "there's been a fight with two women. They are both dead. I have killed them."

It was a tragic end to a bizarre relationship. Albert Goozee was subsequently brought to trial and found guilty of murder. The Leakeys' lodger was sentenced to death. This sentence was later commuted to life imprisonment.

35
MURDER AT ARMLEY FAIR

Jane Banham should have never left the circus. She certainly shouldn't have left it to wed John Hannah, a Manchester tailor. Domesticity did not suit her. Almost before the ceremony was over she was yearning to return to the excitement of the show booth, and within three years she had finally gone. Taking her two children with her, she walked out on her husband and went to live with her father in Blackburn. There she became equestrienne, singer, principal dancer and leading actress in Sam Wild's touring theatrical company.

John Hannah, however, was not a man to relinquish his woman easily. On September 11th, 1856, having heard that the company was at the annual fair at Armley, Leeds, he set off on her trail to plead with her to return home.

On his arrival John Hannah sent Jane a message asking her to meet him at the Malt Mill Inn. To this Jane consented, and accompanied by her father and children, she arrived at the public house shortly before midday. John Hannah was waiting for her in the parlour.

He urged Jane to return to Manchester with him and bring their two children home, but she refused. Jane's father then left the inn, taking the younger child with him.

Minutes later, screams were heard coming from the parlour. When the landlord, George Bird, opened the door, he saw that the tables and chairs had been up-turned. Mrs Hannah's skirt, shawl and bonnet had been scattered and her husband's overcoat was on a seat, covered with blood, which also saturated the floor.

Jane Hannah lay on the floor, with her husband sitting astride her. In his hand was a razor with which he was busily jabbing at her throat. Nearby, paralysed with fear, stood their three-year-old child, splattered from head to toe with his mother's blood.

George Rickards, an Armley surgeon, arrived 20 minutes later. Jane Hannah had a gash across her throat, commencing behind the left ear, and terminating on the right side of her vertebrae. The wound, which extended round three-quarters of her neck, was eleven inches long, and the jugular vein was completely severed. Checking her pulse, he found it very weak.

Although the doctor did all he could to stem the bleeding, Jane Hannah died at about two o'clock that afternoon.

Meanwhile John Hannah had been apprehended. After leaving the Malt Mill he ran towards Leeds, pursued by neighbours and members of the theatre company, and was eventually caught in the grounds of Castleton Lodge Asylum. Taken to Armley's Bay Horse Inn, he was arrested there by Police Constable Joseph Haley, who took him to the Leeds Court House to appear, still wearing his bloodstained coat, before local magistrates: "I had no intention to commit any crime," he blurted out, "I loved her and my children dearly."

At his subsequent trial the court listened with sympathy to the man's story, but they still judged him guilty. As the sentence of death was passed Hannah collapsed in the dock and was removed in a state of unconsciousness.

John Hannah was hanged before a silent and solemn crowd on December 27th, 1856.

36
PASSION IN WIGAN

In 1916 18-year-old Edith Horrocks was working in a munitions factory in Wigan and met Jim Winstanley, a 20-year-old miner. It was with him that Edith had her first experience of sex and she found it magical. The couple were not well suited. They rowed continually, but once in the bedroom everything was put to rights.

After the war ended the factory closed and Edith found work as a barmaid at the Black House in Elliot Street, Wigan. She was still dating Winstanley but she now also made the acquaintance of handsome Harry Taylor. Though a tamer lover, Harry was a better prospect and he soon replaced the miner in her affections.

This may have been a mistake, for whilst Harry was less athletic he was clearly more virile and Edith soon found herself pregnant. At first Harry promised to marry her, and preparations for the wedding began. But then he had second thoughts, saying he was too young to be tied down. Not surprisingly, this news did not go down well with Edith's family, particularly with her mother. She was furious. She told Edith that if she ever saw Harry Taylor again, she would no longer be welcome under her mother's roof.

Reluctant to give Harry up, Edith went to live with her more liberal-minded aunt, and it was at her house in Beech Hill, Wigan, in April 1920 that she gave birth to a daughter. Taylor might have been expected to abandon her, but he didn't. Though he still refused to marry Edith, he made regular payments for the child's upkeep, and also gave Edith some money for herself.

In 1922, however, Edith feared all that would come to an end. Harry announced that he was planning to emigrate to America and seek his fortune. He promised Edith he would still send money for herself and their child, but she found it hard to believe him. Even though the payments continued to arrive, she was still distraught. She was convinced that Harry would eventually forget her and she would end up an old maid.

It was whilst Edith was still fretting over her future that Jim Winstanley walked back into her life. Her old lover looked thin and dejected. He had lost his job and was clearly down on his luck. But Edith was still pleased to see him. Before long Edith and Winstanley were together again and enjoying an even greater passion than they had known before.

"I don't know what has come over me lately," wrote Edith, "but, Jim, you don't realise how much I really love you. Why , Jim, I would give my life for you..."

Even as her new affair was blossoming, Harry was still writing and sending money. But then in October 1923, just as Edith had always feared, his letters stopped. It was exactly as she had predicted, and Edith thanked her lucky stars that Winstanley was now back in her life. Perhaps he was the better catch after all.

In April 1924, however, Harry wrote again. He told her that he was doing very well in his new country. He also declared that they could now be married. He enclosed money for passage and an additional £10. He expected Edith and their daughter to join him as soon as they could.

Not so long ago this would have been the answer to all Edith's dreams, but now that she had fallen in love with Winstanley all over again, she had a difficult and painful decision to make. After much soul-searching she decided that her first duty was to her daughter, and for her sake she would join Harry in America. Edith thus began making arrangements for her journey. She parted with Winstanley and began to pack her bags.

In the following month, however, the United States passed a new quota, halving the number of immigrants allowed into the country. This meant that Edith could not travel at once. It would prove a fatal delay.

Although Edith had said goodbye to Winstanley he refused to give her up. He was forever hanging around her aunt's house, watching and waiting for her. Her aunt, like the rest of Edith's family, wholeheartedly supported her niece's decision to join Taylor in America, and was annoyed by Winstanley's interference. But as time passed and there were more delays in her plans to emigrate, Edith could resist no longer. She began meeting Winstanley again.

Who knows what was going through Edith's mind as she lay in Winstanley's arms? She was still supposed to be travelling to America. Harry was still writing and sending her money. But that seemed to mean nothing. Winstanley asked her to write to Harry and tell him she was seeing another man. She said she would, but that letter was never received. In the meantime Edith passed the letters she received from Harry straight on to Winstanley.

As pressure from her family mounted Edith left her aunt's home to take a live-in job as a barmaid at the Shakespeare Hotel in King Street, Wigan. Presumably she hoped this would make her meetings with Winstanley easier. Unfortunately, as the pub's landlord took a dislike to her boyfriend, the new arrangement made scant difference. But she continued her affair all the same.

However, on Thursday, May 7th, 1925, she saw Winstanley for the very last time. The couple met at six o'clock in the Bridgewater Arms, a pub some distance from Wigan on the road to Shevington, and during the course of the evening visited a number of other pubs. They ended up at the Navigation Inn and from there Edith went no further. Jim Winstanley put his hands round her neck and strangled her.

No one knows what drove Winstanley to murder. Could it have been that Edith chose that evening to tell him she was now really going to America? Was it just the result of another routine argument? Or was it, as Winstanley claimed, because she begged him to do it?

When the police accused Winstanley he made no attempts to deny the killing . "I won't run away," he said. "I am not afraid to die. I will show you where she is. She is dead enough. I throttled her at about midnight."

He then accompanied the detectives to The Navigation. When they reached the spot where her body lay he became hysterical.

"There she is! I want to kiss her!" he cried, falling on his knees at Edith's side. "We used to come here always," he murmured as he tenderly brushed the hair from her face.

Winstanley said that they had made love just before he strangled her. The detectives, however, wondered if Edith had been raped, as they discovered her torn knickers slung over some bushes a few yards away.

On being formally remanded in custody at the police court, Winstanley said only: "It's all right, hang me." At his trial, however, he pleaded not guilty. The jury took just twenty-five minutes to deliver its verdict.

Jim Winstanley was hanged at Walton Prison, Liverpool, on the morning of August 5th, 1925.

37
RUTH ELLIS

Ruth Ellis was not the bright young thing she had wanted to be, but she was a success of sorts. A dyed-blonde small-time model and part-time prostitute, she was by the age of 24 the manageress of a Knightsbridge night-club, the Little Club, in Brompton Road. On a basic £15 a week salary plus a £10 a week entertainment allowance, and a rent-free flat above the club, she was doing pretty well.

It was at the Little Club, one afternoon in 1953, that Ruth met up with the young David Blakely, a 24-year-old doctor's son who was currently working his way through a small £7,000 inheritance and harbouring the ambition to become a racing driver.

She had met him a couple of weeks earlier in another club in the West End and had not been much impressed. Hearing him making some pompous remarks about the hostess there, she told him he was "a pompous ass". Later, to her friends, she described him as "a little shit". But now, serving him a gin and tonic in her own club, that initial antipathy seemed to melt away.

To Ruth Ellis, Blakely represented everything she wanted. He was undeniably posh and well-spoken. He also moved in the right circles. He had neither the ability nor the wealth to make much of an impact on the racing circuit, but that didn't seem to matter. The fact was, he did have a racing car and he did race in France. He was also engaged to an heiress.

The glamour of racing at Le Mans and mixing with the rich set was not lost on the impressionable young woman. It was the dream that she had always craved. With David Blakely, she thought, she might finally achieve it.

Soon she was taking Blakely to bed in her flat above the club, spending lazy sensuous afternoons with him. Not every afternoon, of course, because sometimes Ruth made use of her free afternoons before the club opened to promote her call-girl career. But they were together as often as not. Blakely's supposed fiancée was no problem. He had no intention of marrying her, he said, he was just in it for the money.

Those initial weeks of their relationship were happy times and their romance blossomed. But this was not to last. In December 1953 Ruth discovered she was pregnant and from that moment on their love affair soured. Blakely insisted that he was prepared to marry her, that she didn't need get rid of the child. But he didn't insist nearly hard enough. Ruth never really thought he was sincere. She thus decided on abortion.

Ruth Ellis declared then and later that the abortion did not matter, but she was clearly hurt by the episode. So much so, in fact, that after the abortion she began denying Blakely the exclusive free right to her body. Instead she began encouraging the attentions of Desmond Cussen, a 33-year-old divorced company director, who fell deeply in love with her.

This new liaison was well timed. Cussen was a wealthy man, and with profits at the Little Club slipping, a good insurance policy. When the inevitable happened and Ruth was fired from her job, Cussen seemed a godsend. She moved in with him and they set up home together.

Understandably enough, Blakely was less than enthusiastic about the arrangement. He felt rejected and hurt. He also felt extremely jealous. Now, whenever they met, they would row. But they still continued to meet. They seemed to be addicted to each other.

Perhaps the courtship with Cussen was an elaborate plan by Ruth to trap her real lover for good. If it was, it worked extremely well. Blakely was soon begging her to leave her company director and marry him. Ruth refused, but all the same, in February 1955 she did move out from Cussen's home and she and Blakely took the lease on a modest one-room flat at 44 Egerton Gardens. There they lived together as "Mr and Mrs Ellis".

Alas, this was not as idyllic as either of them might have hoped. Ruth continued to see Desmond Cussen, who was lending her cash to pay the rent. Blakely was also spending time with other women, and at the same time falling more and more into debt and drinking heavily. To cap it all Ruth had a young son, Andy. She had previously kept him more or less out of the way. But now the ten-year-old boy was living with them and adding to the tension.

It was just before Easter 1955 that things finally came to a head. Ruth announced she was pregnant once again. This time, though, she was unable to name the father. It might be Blakely but it could equally well be Cussen.

David Blakely was enraged. Already the worse for drink, he turned on Ruth and punched her in the stomach, causing a miscarriage.

It was the most violent episode in an already violent and tempestuous relationship. But in spite of this, the pair stayed together. In fact it seems as though the fight was quickly forgotten. Shortly afterwards Ruth was again demanding sex from her lover and forcing herself into his arms. Blakely duly obliged. But not for long. On April 8th, 1955, he said he wanted a break from her. That evening he got up and walked out.

Blakely went to visit some friends, Anthony and Carole Findlater. He complained to them that he could stand it no longer and that he and Ruth were now finished. The young couple tried to soothe his fears and calm him down. They also persuaded him to spend the weekend with them at their flat in Tanza Road, Hampstead.

Ruth was expecting Blakely to return home. When he failed to do so she phoned his friends.

"Anthony, is David with you?"

"No," lied Anthony.

"Oh. I'm very worried because he should have been back. Do you think he is all right?"

"Oh, he's all right," said Findlater.

Ruth put down the receiver, convinced that she had detected a mocking note in Anthony's voice and suspecting that Blakely was with the couple.

She rang several more times that night, but as soon as her voice was recognised, the receiver was replaced. Filled with anger, Ruth called Desmond Cussen and got him to drive her to the Findlaters' flat. She rang the bell, but got no answer. Then she spotted her boyfriend's van parked outside. Infuriated, she turned her rage on the van, smashing all its windows. This brought Anthony Findlater to his doorstep.

"Where is David?" Ruth demanded.

Findlater, still in his pyjamas, told her to calm down. He persisted in saying that Blakely wasn't there and then went back inside to call the police.

Ruth spent the whole night waiting outside and keeping watch. The police came and asked her to go, but she wouldn't be persuaded and they couldn't force her. Eventually they went away. No mention was made of her vandalism.

At eight the next morning Findlater and Blakely came out of the flat but did not spot her. They walked over to the van, inspected the damage, then got in and drove away. Ruth too now departed.

That same afternoon however, she was back in Hampstead. By now Ruth was convinced that not only were the Findlaters trying to break up her relationship with

Omaima Nelson (left) murdered her husband, William, on their honeymoon. She dissected his body, some of which she cooked on a barbecue. It was so sweet, she said, so delicious. "I like him tender"

Some of William Nelson's remains, (above) including his genitals, were later found by the police

Reconstructed body of William Nelson on the pathologist's slab

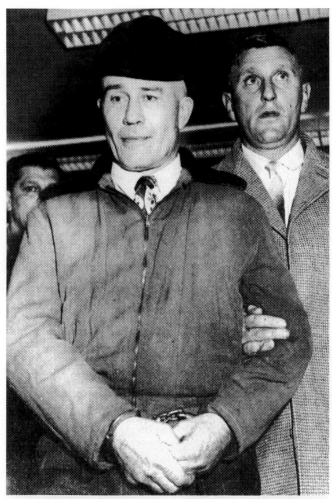

Edward Gein, the inspiration for the film *Psycho*, stands out as a unique gargoyle. Wearing and caressing human remains gave him inexplicable thrills. To Gein the sexual organs of female corpses seemed like living things

The farmhouse (above) where Edward Gein carried out his gruesome dissection of female corpses. It was also here where he mutilated Bernice Worden

The eviscerated and decapitated body of Bernice Worden, hanging from a beam in the ceiling

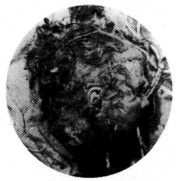

One of Gein's shrunken heads. He would peel off the face and scalp and stuff the heads with newspaper

Denise Labbé and Jacques Algarron. Utterly besotted by her lover and totally under his spell, Denise agreed to his sinister request that she murder her two-year-old daughter and prove her love.

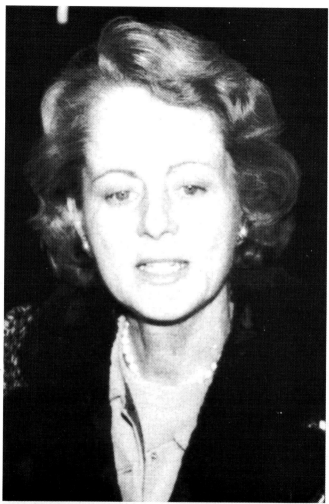

Wild with jealousy and resentment, Jean Harris murdered her long-standing lover Dr Herman Tarnower, when he began an affair with a younger woman. She gave herself up immediately, claiming that she intended to commit suicide in front of him. The murder had been an accident

Mass poisoner Rhonda Belle Martin murdered her husband then married her stepson. She was caught only after she tried to kill him too

Plagued by feelings of inadequacy, Reginald Christie was able to satisfy his sexual longings only by murdering prostitutes and then having intercourse with the corpses

The body of Hectorina MacLennan after removal from Christie's kitchen cupboard. She was the last woman to die

The insatiable sexual appetite of Alberto DeSalvo, the Boston Strangler, led to numerous rapes, countless assaults and a total of thirteen murders in the early 1960s

Blakely but they had also found him a new lover their nanny. She waited angrily outside the flat and kept her vigil until the early hours of Sunday morning. Finally, however, she gave up and returned home. She tried once more to speak to Blakely on the phone but without success.

The following day, Easter Sunday, Ruth was almost out of her mind with jealousy and frustration. Again she went to Hampstead to keep a vigil outside the Findlaters' flat but now the situation was worse than ever. There was a party going on in the flat and Ruth was enraged to hear the sound of a woman's laughter. She was certain it was her rival.

At about 9 o'clock that evening David Blakely and his friend Clive Gunnell popped out of the Findlaters' home and went down to the local pub to get some beer and cigarettes. The Magdala was packed, and the two men had only a quick drink at the bar before buying the beer to take home. Then they said a few goodbyes and left, making for Blakely's van, which was parked outside.

Gunnell waited by the passenger door, while Blakely walked around the vehicle and stood by the driver's door, juggling with his flagons of beer and trying to fish the car keys out of his pocket. They were both too busy to notice the slight but determined blonde walking towards them.

Ruth's eyes were fixed on Blakely. She called out "David" but he did not hear. It was only when she was standing beside him that he noticed her presence.

No words were spoken: it had gone too far for that. Blakely watched almost hypnotized as Ruth Ellis opened her handbag and took out a Smith & Wesson .38 revolver. Raising the weapon, she pointed it at him, saying nothing.

Blakely turned and started to run towards the back of the van. Ellis fired two shots in quick succession. Blakely stumbled, crashing into the side of the van and then stumbling forward.

Clive Gunnell stood stock-still, frozen in terror as the woman calmly stalked her victim. Ruth walked the length of the blood-smeared van to find Blakely scrambling desperately on the other side. She spoke just once. "Get out of the way, Clive," she warned.

She fired again and Blakely's body made a half-turn as it spun sideways. She strode up to the body, firing more shots into it until the six-chamber gun clicked empty. Then she stood like a robot which had been switched off and robbed of purpose. She did not hear the cry of pain from a bank official's wife, Mrs Gladys Yule, who had been wounded in the hand by a ricochet from one of the bullets.

Blakely lay dead in the gutter, a mixture of blood and beer from the smashed flagons coursing towards the drain. Customers had poured out of the Magdala, aroused by the sound of the shots. They stared at the body in amazement. Everyone was in a state of shock. Such things belonged to gangster films: they had no place in Hampstead in 1955.

One of the group looked towards the motionless woman who still clutched the gun. "What have you done?" he screamed. Ruth Ellis made no reply.

A tall, well-built man came out of the Magdala and approached her cautiously. She glanced at him, then said calmly: "Phone the police."

The man studied her for a moment, puzzled by her apparent lack of concern. "I am a police officer," he replied, taking the gun from her hand. Ruth made no effort to resist him, and stood quietly beside Police Constable Alan Thompson.

An ambulance arrived and took away the body. It was followed shortly afterwards by a police car, and Ruth Ellis was driven to Hampstead police station, Police Constable Thompson still beside her.

At the station Ruth Ellis was given a cup of tea. It was

thought she might be in shock. But she remained unmoved, drained of all emotion. She sipped the tea and told the officers in a dull monotone. "My name is Mrs Ruth Ellis. I am a model. I'm 28 and I live at 44 Egerton Gardens, that's in Kensington."

Ruth Ellis was treated kindly by the police and she did her best to explain her crime. She described her feelings of betrayal and frustration, how she felt abandoned and alone. All she would reveal about her gun, however, was that she had been given it a few years ago as security for a small loan. The police suspected she was covering up for someone and told her they did not believe this story. But Ruth said nothing more. Subsequently she would say that the gun had, in fact, been given to her by Desmond Cussen but the claim was never proven.

On Monday, June 20th, 1955, Ruth Ellis stood in the dock at the Old Bailey. She made no attempt to deny the charge of murder. Asked if she intended to kill Blakely, she replied simply: "It is obvious that when I shot him I intended to kill him."

Ruth's counsel stressed the fact that the defendant was under considerable emotional strain at the time, and was in a jealous rage. But he had to admit that, in law, she had been sane. The prosecution counsel agreed.

Stressing that *crime passionel* was not recognised in English law, he said: "I accept fully that there is evidence that this woman was disgracefully treated. I accept it would lend to lead her into an emotional condition." But, whatever the emotional upset, counsel continued, the fact remained that Blakely had been unarmed and defenceless, and the trigger had to be pulled each time for a shot to be fired – six instances of premeditation."

Summing up, the judge told the jury that, given the statement of intent, they could not return a verdict of manslaughter. It would have to be murder. And, he added, "if you are satisfied that Mrs Ellis deliberately fired the shots at Blakely, and as a result of the shots he died, it is not open to you in this case to bring in a verdict of not guilty."

The jury took twenty-three minutes to reach the only verdict possible.

As the black cap was placed on the judge's head and he pronounced the death sentence, Ruth appeared unmoved. When he had finished speaking, she murmured a brief "Thanks" and then turned and smiled to her friends in the public gallery. The decision of death having now been made, Ruth Ellis was led to the cells below, her high heels clicking and her blonde hair catching the last rays of sunlight as she disappeared.

There were petitions, of course, and loud cries of protest. But the government refused to question the court's decision. The fact that an innocent bystander had also been hurt in the incident meant that the pleas for clemency were largely ignored.

On the morning of her death, July 13th, 1955, Ruth Ellis took communion from a Catholic priest, whilst outside the prison a crowd of over a thousand protesters had gathered.

When the final moment came she showed no fear. In her cell she drank the tot of brandy she was offered with a steady hand and thanked the prison staff for the kindness they had shown her. Then she almost hurried from her cell to the execution chamber.

Ruth Ellis was the last woman to be hanged in England. Ten years later, in November 1965, capital punishment in Britain was finally abolished.

38

THOMPSON AND BYWATERS

On the night of October 4th, 1922, having enjoyed
a pleasant evening at the theatre, Edith and Percy
Thompson were returning to their home in Ilford, Essex,
when a man jumped out from the shadows. Brandishing
a knife, the man thrust it into Percy's chest. Percy collapsed to the floor. Edith screamed and cried for help.
But it was too late. By the time help arrived the assailant
had fled and Percy was dead.

The following day Edith was still hysterical and unable to recall anything but the barest details of the attack. She said she had no idea what had happened, or
any idea why. A neighbour of the Thompsons', however,
had been more forthcoming. He told the police that all
had not been well with Edith's marriage and he gave
them the name of Edith's supposed lover: Frederick
Bywaters.

Edith Thompson and Freddy Bywaters had become
lovers the previous summer when the 18-year-old sailor
had accompanied Edith and her husband on a holiday to
the Isle of Wight. It began innocently enough, but the
mutual attraction between Edith and Freddy soon
became a full-blooded passion. In the months that followed the couple were together at every opportunity,
and when Bywaters was away at sea Edith inundated

him with love letters.

These letters, which would eventually condemn Edith Thompson to death, were found when Bywaters was arrested. Amidst all her tender endearments and loving fantasies, Edith had written at length about taking her husband's life. She had, she wrote, already tried it with broken glass, "big pieces, too – not powdered," though this clearly had failed. So how about poisoned chocolates? Or opium?

Edith and Bywaters were arrested on the same day. It was Edith who cracked first, admitting that the man who stabbed her husband had been her lover. Soon afterwards Bywaters also confessed.

The couple were tried at the Old Bailey in December 1922. Edith was accused of inciting Bywaters to murder, a charge which the prosecution supported by quoting revealing extracts from her letters. In the most damning she had written "Yes, darling, you are jealous of him but I want you to be: he has the right by law, to all that you have the right to by nature and love. Yes, darling, be jealous, so much that you will do something desperate."

Throughout the trial Bywaters insisted that there had been nothing in the letters that had incited him to violence. The attack, he said, was in self-defence and in no way premeditated. The jury, however, was not convinced. After two hours, both the defendants were found guilty of murder.

Edith Thompson and Frederick Bywaters were hanged at 9 o'clock in the morning on January 9th, 1923, she at Holloway Prison, he a short distance away at Pentonville.

39
45 MINUTES TO DIE

Mrs Christabell Sharpe lived with her daughter, Mrs Charles Lanier, at 306 Emma Street, Thomasville, North Carolina. On Thursday night, April 12th, 1951, the two women were sitting in the kitchen of their home. Mrs Sharpe held her daughter's baby on her lap. It was 7.55, soon time for the child to be put to bed.

The telephone rang and, still holding the baby, Mrs Sharpe went out to the hall to answer it. She was on the phone for only a few minutes. When she returned she looked pale and shaken.

"He couldn't mean it," she muttered to herself.

"Mean what?" asked her daughter.

"He said he couldn't stand me going out with other men. He had to see me right away. He said if I didn't let him come over, I'd be sorry. Then he said..." Mrs Sharpe hesitated. "He said no matter what happened he was going to kill himself at exactly nine o'clock tonight."

"But who was it?"

The baby began to cry. Mrs Lanier went across and took her from her mother. It was 8 o'clock and time to put the little girl to bed. Mrs Lanier carried her into the adjoining bedroom and tucked her into the crib, then went back into the kitchen and sat down.

"Who was it?" she repeated.

"You don't know him," her mother said. "His name ..."

At that moment there was a sudden, deafening crack, followed by the sound of shattering glass.

Christabell Sharpe groaned and began to walk across the kitchen floor. Her steps grew jerky and at the bedroom door she crumpled and fell.

"Mother!" her daughter screamed. She ran and knelt beside the prostrate woman. A thick trail of crimson, bright against the light-coloured linoleum, trickled from under the body.

Mrs Lanier looked dazedly at the broken pane of glass, then back at the body of her mother. She realised with a sickening sense of fear what had happened. The shot had come through the kitchen window and the killer might still be there, aiming at her. She gasped and fled the room. She grabbed the phone in the hall and implored the operator to send the police.

Police Chief Paul Shore arrived at the Lanier house within seven minutes of her call. He listened patiently to the woman's story. In the meantime a doctor examined Mrs Sharpe's body. A bullet had pierced her lung and nicked the wall of her heart. She would have died almost instantly.

Chief Shore listened with interest as Mrs Lanier told him about the phone call and the evident intention of the killer to die at 9 o'clock.

"He'll do it, too," he said, "If he was desperate to take his own life as a rejected suitor, he'll be more determined now that he's a killer. And I want him alive."

It was 8.15. There were 45 minutes to go.

The police chief now began to question Mrs Lanier.

"How long was it," he asked, "from the time your mother hung up until she was shot?"

"I don't know," the woman replied.

"Come on now," pressed the detective, "try and recall your conversation with her. How long did it take for her to come back from the phone? What did she do between that time and the time of the shot?"

"I'm not sure. I can't remember," Mrs Lanier replied.

"Go to the phone," Shore pleaded. "Hang it up, then try and do exactly what your mother did. Don't walk any faster or any slower. Repeat what both of you said and did. Repeat anything that took up some time."

Mrs Lanier went to the phone and picked up the receiver. As she replaced it Shore glanced at his watch.

Mrs Lanier walked slowly back to her mother's chair. She sat down. Then, in a macabre re-enactment of what had happened barely 30 minutes before, she tried to repeat every word she and her mother had exchanged and every action they had carried out. Suddenly she stopped.

"It was then that we heard the shot!" she exclaimed.

The detective looked back at his watch. "Four minutes, twenty seconds," he said. "The killer must have called from a booth about four minutes away from here!"

At 8.55 p.m. detectives were gathered inside a bar, three blocks away from the Lanier house. It was the only place within the distance that housed a phone booth. The killer, reasoned Shore, must have phoned from here. He might still be inside.

Shore inspected the men at the bar. There was one couple, an old man and a group of five youths in their 20s. The chief felt sure the wanted man was not one of them. Four other men were at tables around the room. One of them was tall and grey-haired. He had a long nose and heavy eyebrows. The half-pint glass of beer that stood in front of him had long gone flat. Next there was a short, stumpy man in his late fifties. He was dressed like a labourer and he gripped his beer glass in quiet desperation. An empty whisky glass stood beside it.

At the other end of the room was a dapper little fellow in his forties dressed in blue serge shirt with a bright red tie. He wore rimless glasses and a Homburg hat set at a jaunty angle on his head. Beside him was a tall man who looked as though he might be a farmer. His florid, flat face was expressionless, his hair yellowed by the sun.

The shirt was so tight it seemed uncomfortable, suggesting he was more used to dungarees and overalls. Had he dressed himself up for a woman?

The minute hand on the wall clock moved towards nine. What would the man do, Shore wondered. The music stopped and the voice of the announcer came over the radio. "You have been listening to..." The minute hand was almost vertical.

"We bring you the latest news," said the voice on the radio. Suddenly the room became strangely still. "Tonight at eight o'clock," the newscaster began, "an unknown assailant fired a shot through a window and killed Mrs Christabell Sharpe. The police ..."

Softly, gently, a man began to cry. Shore leapt to his feet. Which one was it? A flash of metal reflected in the dim lights of the bar as the stumpy labourer raised a gun to his head. Shore made a grab for him and the pistol clattered to the floor.

At his trial Alexander Clodfelter, 59, married and the father of five grown children, admitted his love for Mrs Christabell Sharpe. He also admitted killing her.

"We'd been going together for years," he said, "but nobody knew it. Then she decided she wanted to marry a younger man. I couldn't stand the thought." He had to kill her, he said, then he planned to kill himself.

"I told her I'd do it at nine o'clock," he confessed. "I had a crazy idea that we had a date at that time, and with her dead, I had to be dead too to keep it."

On July 28th, 1951, Alexander Clodfelter was sentenced to life imprisonment.

40

"SOMEBODY'S SHOT BARRY"

Barry Ford hadn't intended to go out that night. He was perfectly happy spending the evening at home, watching television and snuggling up with his pretty 27-year-old wife, Anita. But then the phone rang. A friend wanted a favour, and not being one to let people down, Barry said he would go. He told Linda he'd be back soon. Within the hour, he thought. But Barry Ford never came home.

At 10.40 p.m. on Monday, September 3rd, 1984, a police officer patrolling Huntingdon Beach saw Barry's pick-up in the middle of the street, The motor was running and the headlights were on. He walked over to see what was happening and then stopped in his tracks.

A man was sprawled on the ground, face down. One hand was flopped by his side, the back of his head glistening with fresh blood.

The policeman crouched down and pushed two fingers against the side of the man's neck. He got a pulse. It was weak but the man was still alive.

Within minutes an ambulance was on the scene. An oxygen mask was placed over Barry Ford's mouth and an intravenous tube was inserted into a fresh vein. Seconds later the ambulance was racing towards the hospital.

In the emergency room doctors worked feverishly to

save Barry, but it was no use. He died later that morning without ever regaining consciousness.

Anita answered the knock on the door on Tuesday morning. Trying to break the news as gently as possible, Detective Dale Mason told her that her husband had died in the hospital that night.

Anita gasped in disbelief and stumbled backwards into the living-room. Her jaw dropped and her eyes filled with tears. The detectives comforted her as best they could, but they also needed to ask her some questions.

"Yes," she said. "I understand. But can I call my brother first? He should know."

"Sure, go ahead," said Mason.

With shaking hands, Anita dialled a number and blurted out the bad news. "Somebody's shot Barry," she gasped, "He's dead."

Detective Mason turned to his colleague, who returned his look of surprise. Neither of them had mentioned shooting.

Clearly Anita knew a lot more about her husband's murder than she was letting on. Some digging quickly revealed that she had plenty of motive. Barry had a $140,000 life insurance policy naming her as sole beneficiary. And in the event of his death she also stood to inherit the house, the car and all the family possessions, not to mention her husband's thriving tow-truck business. But to get those things Anita had to act fast.

According to friends, the Ford marriage was on the rocks. Anita had a fiendish alcohol and cocaine problem and it had all but destroyed her relationship with her husband. Barry had already removed her name from their joint bank account and had frozen their credit cards. He had recently been talking about divorce.

But had Anita killed him? It seemed unlikely. The police were sure she was somehow involved, but they doubted that she had pulled the trigger. Who then had shot Barry Ford?

Police learned that in the weeks before the shooting

Anita had approached several people in the bars she frequented and had asked them if they knew where she could hire a hitman. Obviously, someone had taken her seriously. But who? Detectives didn't have an answer to that question until they got a tip that a neighbour of the Fords, Brad Chase, had been seen visiting the Ford home almost daily prior to the shooting.

Chase had already been questioned. A young man with a nervous demeanour, he confirmed he was friendly with Barry Ford. Now, according to the new information, Chase had not only been friends with Barry but also with Anita. It was she whom he had been visiting every day. Brad Chase was brought in for interrogation.

Crippled by a ferocious drug habit, it didn't take much for the young man to blurt out everything. In a detailed statement which he would later repeat in court, Chase said Anita Ford was the mastermind behind the plot to kill Barry and she had persuaded two men to carry out her plan. The gunman was her brother, George Wright. His accomplice was one of the Fords' neighbours, a man who had already described himself as Barry's best buddy: John Aldridge. "With friends like Aldridge," remarked Detective Mason, "you don't need enemies."

Chase said that they had all been sitting around the Ford home, drinking beer and getting high, and the talk had got around to getting rid of Barry, who had already threatened divorce and writing his wife out of the insurance policy. They all agreed that if they were going to do it, it had to be soon.

Chase said they had finally decided to lure Barry from his house on the pretence that Aldridge's car had broken down.

Aldridge phoned the Ford home at around 10 p.m. and asked Barry to come and help him start his car. Chase, who had just gone along for the ride, said that as the two old friends talked George Wright materialised out of the shadows, stuck a gun to the back of Barry's head and fired two shots. Barry dropped like a stone.

Anita Ford was arrested on October 24th, 1984. No one has ever looked more shocked. Taken away in handcuffs, she insisted: "I didn't do it."

A similar statement, peppered with obscenities, was given by Anita's brother, George Wright. "I don't know what the hell this is all about," he shrieked. Also claiming innocence was John Aldridge. They were all charged.

Brad Chase was also charged with murder. However, he was later allowed to plead guilty to the charge of voluntary manslaughter in return for his testimony against the others.

Bright-eyed and drug-free, Chase proved to be a credible witness and absolutely devastating to the defence.

In February 1988 John Aldridge pleaded guilty to murder charges and was sentenced to 15 years to life in state prison. A few months later triggerman George Wright was found guilty of first-degree murder and conspiracy. He was sentenced to life imprisonment.

Of the three, only Anita Ford took the witness stand. At her trial in May 1987 the sultry brunette announced to the jury that her ex-husband had been a bully and a wife-beater. She denied killing him or having any part in the plan.

"Who did then?" her attorney asked.

Anita had an answer, Her brother George, she maintained, didn't like Barry and when he learned that Barry had beaten her he decided to mete out a little justice on his own.

The jury was not convinced. On June 3rd, 1987, Anita Ford was found guilty of conspiracy to murder for financial gain. She was sentenced to life imprisonment.

41
FATAL FLIGHT

On September 9th, 1949, a Canadian Pacific DC-3 en route from Montreal to Baie Comeau exploded in mid-flight and crashed into Mount Torment just outside Quebec. All 23 passengers and crew members were killed.

At first it was thought that the crash had been an accident. The suddenness of the explosion, however, coupled with eye-witness reports from those who had seen the crash, soon suggested that it might have been the result of a bomb on board the plane. It had probably been stored in the freight compartment.

A clerk at Quebec City Airport, where the plane had stopped off, was amongst the first to be questioned. His records contained a brief description of every parcel that had been carried on the ill-fated plane and police investigators were able to contact every shipper except one. The sender of that particular package remained elusive.

The parcel, a "religious statuette" weighing twenty-seven pounds, had been sent by one Dephis Bouchard in Quebec to a certain Alfred Plouffe in Baie Comeau but it was soon found that both these names were fictitious.

Fortunately, however, the airport clerk was able to recall the shipment and shipper fairly well. She was a woman probably in her late twenties, fairly slim and dressed in black. He also remembered that she had arrived at the airport in a taxi.

Every taxi driver in Quebec City was contacted and questioned. Before long one was found who was able to give the police the information they sought. He had picked up a woman answering the clerk's description from Palaise station, and he remembered helping her with the heavy parcel. He had driven her to the airport and then to an address on Rue Monseigneur Gauvreau.

It was not difficult to establish the woman's identity. She was well known in the squalid section of the city where she lived. Her name was Marguerite Pitre. Mme Pitre was in no position to answer the investigators' questions, however. By the time the police had identified her she was in hospital, recovering from a suicide attempt.

Mme Pitre's hospitalization did not suspend the investigation entirely, for the police had already made a careful check on the woman's background and uncovered an interesting fact. Among Marguerite Pitre's acquaintances was a 32-year-old jeweller, one J. Albert Guay. One of the victims of the plane disaster had been Guay's wife, Rita.

Detectives thought it unlikely that an unskilled woman would have been able to assemble a bomb by herself. But a jeweller like Guay, familiar with clocks and watches, could be assumed to possess all the necessary knowledge. He could have constructed the delicate timing mechanism with no difficulty. It was also learned that Guay had once worked in a munitions factory, and thus also had a knowledge of explosives.

By the time Mme Pitre had recovered sufficiently to answer their questions, detectives already had a pretty good idea what had happened. Guay and Pitre were lovers. They had wanted to be rid of his wife, so Guay had constructed the bomb and Pitre had taken it to the airport for it to be loaded on to the plane. They knew that Rita would be on the flight because Guay had bought her ticket. It was a perfect plan. The bomb would bring an end to Rita Guay and provide some insurance money into the bargain.

Once Pitre started talking, however, the police soon realised that things were nothing like as simple as they seemed.

"Yes," Pitre said. She had taken the package to the airport and she later discovered that it had contained a bomb, but she was not Guay's mistress, she was merely his friend.

Marguerite did contribute to Guay's love life but only in so far as she lent him her flat from time to time so he could entertain his various girlfriends. Chief among these was Marie-Ange Robitaille, an alluring 19-year-old waitress who worked in a Quebec nightclub. Marie-Ange and Guay had been lovers since she was fifteen and there had been recent talk of marriage. It was to free himself to marry her that Guay had killed his wife.

The investigators were also mistaken in thinking that Guay had constructed the bomb himself. Although Guay was in the jewellery business, he was not a skilled clockmaker. For several years he had been taking work of this nature to an expert watch repairer, Généreux Ruest. It was Ruest who had constructed the timing mechanism for the bomb, and Ruest just happened to be Marguerite Pitre's brother.

Bizarrely, though Mme Pitre admitted all this, and also said that she had brought the dynamite and the fuses for Guay, she still insisted that she did not know that Guay's wife was on the plane or that the package she had sent air-express on that flight had been a bomb. Guay had said he needed the dynamite for clearing some land and when she took the parcel on to the plane she really believed it was a statue. Only eleven days after the crash, when the newspapers were saying that the police were looking for the woman who had delivered the parcel, did she begin to realise the truth. She had confronted Guay about it.

"But you told me it contained a statue," Marguerite

claimed she said to Guay, "I have done nothing wrong. The police can't be looking for me for that."

"No matter what I said," he told her. "It was a bomb you took to the airport. And if the police can prove it was you, they'll get you and you will hang."

Marguerite Pitre said she was terrified.

"But what can I do?" she pleaded.

"There's only one way out for you" he allegedly said. "You must use those sleeping pills I gave you. Take them all and turn on the gas. You'll not feel a thing that way, but you certainly will if the police get you."

Incredibly, Marguerite took his advice, and hence her sojourn in hospital. But though she had taken enough pills to kill her she had somehow survived.

Guay was promptly arrested and charged with the murder of his wife. Ruest was brought in too.

As the investigators prepared the case for trial they formed the opinion that both Ruest and Pitre had been innocent, though extremely foolish, unknowing accomplices in Guay's murder plot. They deserved a reprimand, but nothing more. It was Guay and Guay alone who was the real villain.

At the trial in February 1950 Guay stood alone in the dock to face the charge of murder. On June 23rd, 1950, Joseph Albert Guay was judged guilty and sentenced to death. He dropped from the scaffold on January 12th, 1951.

Subsequently the police revised their opinion of the relative innocence of Généreux Ruest and Marguerite Pitre. They were no longer regarded as foolish dupes but as co-conspirators in the devilish crime. A year later the police had enough evidence to prove it and the charges were filed.

Ruest was hanged on July 25th, 1952. Pitre followed him into eternity on the morning of January 9th, 1953.

42
THE MISSING WIFE

"There's no reason why she should leave without letting me know," said the worried husband. "The last time I saw her was about six o'clock Monday when I left for work. She hasn't contacted me since, and I can't find anyone who knows where she is or where she might be."

Don and Betty Ann Walkden had been married for seventeen years, and while it hadn't been the most perfect marriage, Betty Ann had never left home before. She had threatened to, Don said, but she had never gone through with it.

The police in Big Spring, Texas, were not too worried by the disappearance. Betty Ann had only been missing for a day and there was no evidence of foul play. She had even packed some of her clothes before going. It seemed a regular domestic walkout. A week later, however, and with still no word from Betty Ann, it was time to make serious inquiries.

On June 29th, 1992, Deputy Eddie Howell met Walkden at the landfill site where he worked.

Donald Walkden repeated what he had told the police earlier. He had arrived home on Tuesday, June 16th, and found that Betty Ann was missing. "There were two suitcases gone, and some of her clothing," he said. "And she took four hundred dollars in cash, but left our cheque book." What was strange, said Walkden, was that he later found her wallet on the ground in front of their house. The wallet contained her driving licence, Social Security card and some other papers.

He had telephoned her family in El Paso, but they hadn't heard from her and neither had her friends. He had also checked all the motels in the area and the local bus station, but hadn't found a single trace of her.

Walkden described his wife as an attractive woman, 35 years old, 5 feet 7 inches tall and weighing 11 stone. She had brown hair and green eyes.

Walkden was clearly upset by his wife's disappearance and urged the detective to find her. But despite this Howell was suspicious. "This guy has killed his wife," was the thought that kept going round in his mind. There was no evidence to back this up, nothing to indicate that Betty Ann Walkden was even dead. All Howell had was a gut feeling.

As time went by Howell's theory began to make more and more sense. Certain things in Walkden's story didn't add up. Furthermore, he had told some blatant lies.

Walkden had said that the $400 his wife had taken was money he had withdrawn from his bank account. But the bank had no record of such a withdrawal. He said that he had contacted Betty Ann's friends, but none of them had heard from him. Neither had the motels he had supposedly called.

When Howell called at Walkden's home his suspicions became even more firmly grounded. Don Walkden was unable to say what clothes Betty Ann had taken with her, and everything still seemed to be in the drawers.

"I guess she just took what she had on," said Walkden.

The deputy noticed that there was only one pillow on the bed.

"Don't you have another pillow?" he asked.

"She must have taken it with her," Walkden replied.

Betty Ann left her underwear but took her pillow? It didn't seem likely. Howell grew a little more hostile.

"We might want you to take a lie detector test," he said, leaving Walkden in no doubt that he was now under suspicion.

A few days later, on July 1st, Howell received a phone call from Walkden. He was phoning from home and crying as he told the officer that he had received a postcard from his wife.

Howell drove to Walkden's home and looked at the card. It was postmarked June 30th and had been mailed from Hobbs, New Mexico. The message, written in a masculine scrawl on the back of the card, read: "I'm sorry but I'm one month pregnant by a friend. We are going to Idaho. By the time you get this I'll be long gone."

The detective was no handwriting expert, but he was pretty certain that the card had been written by Walkden himself. Further study of the postcard and samples of Donald Walkden's script confirmed his theory. Walkden had clearly thought that the postcard would put him in the clear. Instead it did exactly the opposite. Walkden was brought in to the sheriff's office.

"I'm trying to be a friend when I tell you you're going to have to do one of the toughest things you have ever done in your life," said Howell. "You've done something bad and you need to tell us about it and get this thing off your chest."

Then the deputy took a gamble. "I know where you buried your wife because I've been watching you at work. I've seen the spot you keep walking back to several times a day and staring at."

"Really?" Walkden asked. "You've been watching me?"

Howell talked some more about Betty Ann being in the ground, not having a proper burial, that she was loved by her parents and that once Walkden must have loved her too .

Walkden broke down.

At first he said that he had just found his wife's dead

body and had buried her in a panic. But then he admitted the truth. He admitted that he had killed her and volunteered to make a statement.

He said that his marriage had been on the rocks and he had thought about murdering Betty Ann for some time. That night they had had yet another argument.

He had shot her as she lay asleep in bed, he said. She died instantly, he thought, because she never moved. Walkden then wrapped her in the bedsheets, along with her pillow, and carried her to the kitchen table. There he tied a plastic rubbish bag over her head to keep the blood from dripping, took her to his truck and drove to the landfill.

Knowing where the crews would be burying the rubbish bales the next day, he dumped the wrapped body in a space that would be covered with dirt within the next few hours. He watched as the bulldozers unknowingly covered the wrapped body the following morning.

It took nearly twelve hours for Betty Ann's body to be recovered from the tip. By the time it was brought to the surface it was already in an advanced state of decomposition.

On July 8th, 1992, Donald Walkden pleaded guilty to the murder of his wife. He received a prison sentence of 70 years.

43
THE BOASTFUL BLUEBEARD

Personal: Gentleman of striking appearance, courteous, pleasing disposition, well connected in business, has much property, associated with several corporations, has solid bank account, as well as nice supply of government bonds, would be pleased to correspond with refined young lady or widow. Object, matrimony. This advertisement is in good faith. All answers to it will be treated with discretion and respect.

H.L. Gordon, Tacoma Hotel, Tacoma

In the spring of 1919, using a variety of aliases and several hotel addresses, James Watson inserted this advertisement in a number of leading papers in America. Not one word of the advertisement was true, except for "Object, matrimony." But hundreds of lonely women sighed over it and dozens answered.

So many ladies wished to wed the advertiser that Watson had to be careful to sift the merely amorous from the financially well-provided. Portable assets, cash on the line, not youth or charm, were what he wanted. And in the earliest crop of replies there was one who offered just that.

Betty Pryor was from Coeur d'Alene, Idaho. A retired spinster with her own home and a healthy bank account, she was the ideal marriage prospect for Watson. After a brief correspondence he travelled to see her, and incredibly had his proposal of marriage accepted just three days later. They married on March 25th and honeymooned in Seattle straight after.

Watson's success with women was astonishing. He rarely told them the truth. He never gave them his real name. And yet they all fell at his feet. But then James Watson could spin a good yarn. To Betty he said he was an agent for the Secret Service. The President of the United States had personally sworn him in, he revealed. It was scarcely believable, but Betty fell for it. No doubt it helped that Watson was extremely good in bed. Everyone knows that spies make good lovers, though that surely can't be their only qualification. Still, Betty was content.

Being in the Secret Service, however, did have its drawbacks. "I might be called away at any moment," he warned her. Not surprisingly, almost as soon as Betty had granted her husband power-of-attorney over her business interests and had transferred her sizeable bank account into joint names, the call of duty came. Watson left for Vancouver. A dangerous mission, he said, something to do with smuggling.

It wasn't smugglers that Watson encountered in Vancouver, however. It was a wealthy English widow, Beatrice Andrewartha. She was another respondent to his advertisement.

Watson met Beatrice on May 2nd, 1919. He proposed to her on the 5th. A week later, on Monday, May 12th, they were man and wife. But even as they were making ready for the wedding night, Watson had other plans in his mind. One of these was a highly promising letter-writer living in Yakima, Washington state. She was a well-to-do-spinster, Bertha A. Goodnick, and a woman just ripe for plucking.

It was an exacting schedule. James was placating one wife with letters, another with embraces and at the same time keeping their prospective successors ready and waiting. He managed it for a while, but it was exhausting. By early summer he had had enough.

Beatrice had already taken her bridegroom's advice and deposited her savings into their joint account, so Watson knew what to do. He and Beatrice went boating on Lake Washington. Soon afterwards his bride of only eight weeks met with a boating accident. Her disappearance seemed so final and so easy he didn't even bother to report it. Instead he returned smartly to Idaho and to Betty's tender embrace.

By now Betty had lost some of her enthusiasm for the Secret Service. She preferred to have her husband by her side. But her patriotic fervour returned when Watson told her his exciting news.

"I've a grand surprise for you," he said in his most charming manner.

"What now?" Betty demanded, rather sceptically.

Watson was thinking hard. "My new mission," he said, "will start in a week or ten days. And my chief said to me, 'You'd better take a girl operative along next time, to pose as your wife. It will serve as a perfect disguise and cover.' And I said, 'Chief, I know the very girl to take.'"

"But I am your wife!" Betty bristled.

"Of course you are. And now you'll be in the Secret Service too. But you won't have to take any oath," Watson added hastily, seeing Betty's eyes shine in sudden anticipation of a visit to the White House.

On Thursday, June 19th, Watson and the newly enlisted "agent Betty" set forth on their "mission for the United States Government". They travelled for three days, ending up in a remote little place in Ferry County, Washington state, where they registered at a small hotel. Watson suggested that Betty remain in the room while he went out and scouted around.

Later Watson returned, and after an early supper he told his wife that they would have to go for a drive. He drove her to a lonely cabin on a hillside. He had been ordered to keep watch on a certain gang, he revealed, and that was best done from this isolated vantage point.

Exploring the cabin with him, Betty surveyed its long-disused interior with distaste and voiced her tart opinion of such Secret Service duties.

Watson merely smiled. "It's a pity you don't favour this location, my dear. You may stop here for quite a long time," he told her.

"What do you mean by that?" she retorted.

"You have done the unpardonable thing of making a nuisance of yourself. You've nagged me and spied on me, you've even dared to criticise my work. Why, you've made me more trouble than all my other wives put together."

"All your other wives?" Betty gasped.

"Yes. Many. Of whom, my angel, you will be the very first to die in this lonely place."

Watson grabbed hold of a spade and stood between his wife and the door. Betty backed away. Then in stark desperation she rushed towards him, hoping to get past and flee into the night. Watson swung the spade brutally at her face. Betty screamed. Watson swung the spade again, several times, with measured and savage accuracy. Soon afterwards he was making use of it for a more conventional purpose. He was digging his wife's grave.

Later Watson returned to the hotel and informed the owner that Betty had left. "My wife has been called away suddenly," he said. "Serious illness in her family."

Early the following day Watson also left, ostensibly to join his wife. In fact he was heading toward Yakima, Washington, to Bertha Goodnick.

Back at the hotel the puzzled proprietor was following a slow train of thought. He went to the wall phone and called a friend, who was also a deputy sheriff.

"Funny thing out here, Joe," he said. "Thought I ought to tell you. Guy comes here with his wife, a nice-looking young woman. He signs up, saying they are Mr and Mrs Harvey Newton from Seattle. No haggle about the prices either. But then late last evening, he comes back alone and tells me, without my asking, that his wife has just been called away suddenly. Sickness in her family. Well, how could she be called so suddenly when no letter or phone call or telegram came for her here?"

"It could be something," the deputy agreed. "I'll ring the sheriff and ask him if I should look into it."

In the meantime Bertha Goodnick was eagerly awaiting Watson's promised visit. She couldn't help wondering what it was that had made him fall in love with her. How could anybody, just by reading her letters, discover in her such captivating grace and charm, such a natural complement to his own lonesome longing? Despite her misgivings, however, she wasn't going to look a gift horse in the mouth.

Watson duly arrived and, inevitably, swept the poor woman off her feet. They were married on July 30th, and as it took nearly a month for her to complete all the paperwork and sign all the various documents relating to her inheritance, their marriage lasted an unusually long time. But, by the beginning of September everything was in order. It was on September 11th that the tragic mishap occurred and Bertha fell into the swirling waters of the St. Joe River.

Alice Ludvigston was Watson's next wife. They were married on October 6th. This new bride proved to be more vivacious, prettier and far more amorous than her predecessors. But it did her little good. On October 16th, after just ten days of wedlock, another outrageous mischance resulted in her slender, passionate, young body sinking for ever beneath the waters of Lake Washington.

James Watson's courtship of his next bride was the closest he ever came to real affection. Kathryn Hyatt was a tall, blonde beauty, just 29 years old. Watson had travelled all the way to California to meet her but once he did he felt that every mile of his journey had been worth while. James and Kathryn were married on November 17th and this time the killer resolved, or almost resolved, that she would be one wife to whom an accident would not occur.

But though Watson's affection for Kathryn was strong, it wasn't strong enough to stop him chasing other prey. Within a month of their wedding he was off on a "secret mission". This time it was with a wealthy widow from Kentucky, Nina Lee Deloney. They were wed on December 5th, but they parted soon afterwards. Taking her on a trip to Mexico, Watson beat his new wife about the head with a hammer, stripped off her clothes and buried her in the desert. He then rushed back to young Kathryn.

Alas, however, though he had been quick, he had not been quick enough. Kathryn had been worried about him and had already engaged a private detective to check on his well-being. It was as a consequence of this that, when Watson returned to California he found the police waiting on his doorstep.

Their investigations had already revealed some of his crimes. But by the time Watson appeared in court the list had grown considerably. It was revealed he had bigamously married no fewer than 29 times, murdered at least five women and amassed a fortune totalling more than $100,000.

At his trial James Watson expressed utter contempt for the women he had married and killed. "They were all stupid," he declared, "a pushover for a flossy speech or faked-up lie, dumb as sheep about money."

On May 10th, 1920, James Watson was sentenced to life imprisonment.

Watson arrived in San Quentin on May 18th, 1920. The callous murderer seemed racked with fear, and with good reason. Convicts have little respect for wife-killers. Many inmates felt that a life sentence for multiple murder was unfair. They cursed him and spat on his face.

For his protection, James Watson was given a job as an orderly in the tuberculosis ward. Eventually he contracted the disease himself and died on October 15th, 1939.

44

CORA'S REVENGE

Cora Cable possessed an ethereal beauty that took men's breath away. Her home in Clinton, Illinois, was a popular rendezvous in the 1890s for every eligible young blade in the county. At the merest flick of her dainty hand any man in town would have been hers for the asking.

Cora had finished high school and was about to begin her freshman year at Champaign University. But she didn't remain there long. On one of her holiday trips home she met a handsome youth at a church social who dazzled her with his extravagant tales of life as it is lived in the big cities; in New York, Paris, Singapore, Cape Town. He claimed to have visited them all.

"Cora," he murmured, "you're too beautiful to waste yourself on all this. Come away with me tonight. We'll be married. We'll see all those glorious things that up to now you've only read or dreamed about."

It was then that Cora Cable made the most foolish decision of her life. She agreed to her suitor's crazy plan. She consented to become Sam Sullivan's wife. They were married that same night by a sleepy-eyed justice of the peace and took an early morning train for St. Louis to begin their honeymoon.

To start with, everything was wonderful. The 18-year-old Cora marvelled at the luxury of their hotel and revelled in her new independence. For the first time in her life she felt really free. Alas, however, this blissful state of affairs was not to last.

Three weeks later Cora sat on the bed in her expensive hotel suite and cried bitter and hopeless tears. Beside her lolled the man she had married such a short time before, a derisive smirk across his face.

"So you're too good to do me a little favour, eh? You, the girl who talked about burning bridges and daring anything. Bah! You're just a snivelling little child. What a fool I've been, wasting three good weeks on you."

Sullivan got up, strode barefoot around the room, lit a cigarette and then put it out after taking three puffs. "I tell you," he shouted, levelling a finger at the cringing girl, "you do what I say without any more fuss or, by heaven, I'll make you wish you'd never been born a woman! We need money, and plenty of it. And it's up to you to make it!"

Cora buried her face deeper into her hands. "Oh, Sam, how could you ask me to do this horrible thing? I won't walk the streets, I tell you. I'll kill myself first!"

Something akin to bewilderment flashed across Sullivan's face. His lips tightened. In an annoyed tone he exclaimed, "All right, all right! Pack your bags and get out of here. Maybe I'm getting soft..."

Sullivan dressed, then went to the door. "I'm going out," he said, "and when I come back you'd better be gone. Understand? I mean what I say."

So Cora Sullivan was left heartbroken and well-nigh penniless in St. Louis. What was she to do? She could not bring herself to return home to Clinton. She had written too many letters telling of her fine husband, boasting of the glorious future in store for them. The disgrace, the gossip, would be more than she could bear.

Cora thus resolved to stay in St. Louis. But never again would she risk being mistreated and abandoned. She had played fair with a man and had been cruelly betrayed. Now she would even the score.

The disillusioned young woman spent the next six years perfecting her technique for making men do her bidding: persuading them to buy clothing to enhance her slender figure and jewellery to glitter at her throat. She did not follow the vocation her husband proposed for her. Cora was never a common prostitute. But her work was much the same; she just charged a higher price.

In 1902 Cora met Guy Wayne Butts, a rising young property developer. For Butts a romantic liaison was not enough. Marriage was the only proposition he would listen to. Cora knew that such a marriage would not be legal, as she was still married to the rascal Sullivan. But she went through with the ceremony all the same.

The marriage was not a success but it was profitable. When they divorced five years later Cora emerged with some $10,000 and an attractive cottage. Now, with money and a home of her own, Cora could live exactly as she wanted. She made the fullest use of all her charms, bewitching men from all around.

Time passed. At 30 Cora had lost none of her youthful beauty. At 40, thanks to the meticulous care that she took of herself, she still could pass for a woman of 25. Men were still willing to pay for her charms.

It was only after her forty-first birthday that Cora finally let her icy heart thaw. It was then that Eduardo Treuba, a wealthy Mexican landowner met her and fell madly in love with her. Soon he was proposing marriage. For once Cora did not make him play the dupe. Here was something deep, something real. It was a new sensation. The Mexican was handsome, far better-looking than Sullivan had been. And he was genuinely in love.

"I'll have to think it over, Eduardo," she said.

"But you must not think it over, my sweet. You must come away with me now, to Mexico City!" His dark eyes sparkled with eagerness. "There I will be the envy of all my friends. They will say, 'This Eduardo, he is one lucky man! Has he not brought back the fairest señora in all

America?' I will not take no for an answer! At least you will take a trip to Mexico City with me?"

Cora thought long and hard about the proposal and finally she agreed.

"Yes, I have always wanted to see Mexico..."

Two years later, back in St. Louis once more, Mr and Mrs Eduardo Treuba were living in a house at 4312 North Broadway. Their marriage had evidently been a success. The two were joyful and content. But there remained one cloud in Cora's otherwise blue sky for she knew she was not legally married. The ceremony had been nothing more than a sham. She resolved this would have to change.

Cora decided that there was only one thing to be done. She must find Sam Sullivan, wherever he might be, and straighten out the tangled skein of her life. Perhaps they could arrange a quiet divorce in another state. After that she would persuade Treuba to remarry her. Perhaps she could say that she wanted to be married again under Mexican law.

Cora advertised discreetly in the newspapers, asking for Sam Sullivan to come forward. As a result, one evening in early spring 1931, a tall, emaciated, silver-haired stranger knocked on her door. Coolly the man walked inside.

"Nice place you've got here, lady. I believe I'm going to like it," he said.

He chose a comfortable chair, drew out a cigar and lit it.

"Just who are you?" demanded Mrs Treuba. "What do you want?"

"Now, Cora, is that the way to talk to your husband? As for my name, it's William Hebner. Don't you remember? I went under the name of Samuel Sullivan when we first met all those years ago. But I've decided to use my real name now. But Hebner or Sullivan, I'm still your lawfully wedded husband, and don't you forget it."

Cora's husband had seen her advertisement and learnt of her new-found happiness. He had now returned to claim his due. But it wasn't to be as simple as Cora had thought. He wasn't going to be fobbed off with money and gifts.

"No, I won't divorce you, Cora," he declared. "I'd be a fool to do that."

William Hebner then delivered his ultimatum. She was to leave Treuba within two weeks, he said. Then she was to join him, giving him her money, her property and all she possessed. If she did not he would expose her to Treuba and bring scandal down on both their heads.

Sick with despair, Cora considered his words. She could not bring herself to confess all to her present husband and beg forgiveness. The sensitive Mexican, she knew, could never endure such a revelation. There was nothing else to do but agree to Hebner's proposal.

Working desperately against time, Cora acted her part skilfully. She told Eduardo that she no longer loved him and wanted a divorce. She further requested that he should return to Mexico and never bother her again.

It was a bitter pill to take, and the emotional Mexican's pleas were pitiful to behold. But at last he went, leaving everything behind for the woman he had loved so desperately. Cora never saw him again.

William Hebner now ensconced himself in the home his predecessor had so recently vacated and began to live a life of pleasure. Drinking parties were a nightly occurrence, interspersed with poker and dice games that swiftly drained Cora's comfortable bank account.

As if this were not enough, Hebner also openly consorted with other women, many of them a good deal younger than himself. Once he had the colossal effrontery to bring an 18-year-old girl home with him to spend the night. The next morning he announced to Cora that the girl was his wife! "I married her last night," he said, laughing uproariously. Cora was left with the thankless task of breaking the news to the unfortunate girl.

Things carried on like this for many months. Cora could have escaped, of course. But she choose not to. She had come to accept her husband as a living example of Sinbad's Old Man of the Sea. She believed she would never be rid of him, and after a while, she stopped even trying.

Cora and Hebner eventually moved to a farm in Arkansas, where they made a good living duping many lonely and loveless souls out of money and possessions. They placed advertisements in the "lonely hearts" columns of newspapers and magazines and took the respondents for everything they could get. In the years that followed Hebner went through illegal marriage ceremonies with at least 19 women, draining them all of whatever personal wealth they had before he discarded them.

Records show that Cora "married" only two men, one in 1933 and another three years later. But she consorted with many more, and, whenever she went to visit a man foolish enough to have answered her advertisement she always came home with more money than when she left.

Despite the fortunes that they were both making, however, Hebner was still throwing most of their money away on drink and cards. Soon there was a real danger of the creditors moving in. Thus in 1937 the couple moved once more. They put a deposit on another farmhouse, one in Pocahontas, Arkansas.

They moved to the new farm in the spring of that year, and two months later, in May, William Hebner "made a long trip". Cora said he had gone to Oklahoma on business, but he never came back. Indeed, William Hebner was never seen again.

It was inevitable that, in a small community like Pocahontas, rumours would start. Cora was seen to be a morose and bad-tempered woman of whom all sorts of ill deeds were thought possible, and when her husband left the gossips were quick to suggest that she had killed him. They said she had buried him in the farm's storm cellar.

True, Cora had filled in the cellar. But, as she explained patiently to Sheriff John Thompson, that was because it was about to cave in.

"If you believe the stories, why don't you dig it out and see for yourself, Sheriff?" Cora offered. "I wish you would. Maybe it would stop all this talk."

Sheriff Thompson was nonplussed by this surprising remark and he didn't take her up on the offer. Instead he drove back into town and declared that all the rumours were just malicious gossip.

A year later, however, and the Sheriff had to admit his error. Cora had left the farm and the new tenants had moved in. It was about a week before they decided to excavate the cellar. They found William Hebner's decomposing body a short while later.

Thompson sighed. "So she did do it after all," he said.

A warrant charging Cora Hebner with murder was quickly issued and the hunt for the woman began.

Cora was eventually tracked down to a house in Miami, where she was living with an elderly man with whom she had been corresponding. They were planning to get married.

Cora insisted that she was utterly innocent of all charges. Indeed, she declared that her husband was not dead at all. Whoever it was that they found in the cellar had had nothing to do with her. All the same, she was taken into custody.

She arrived back in Pocahontas on March 21st, 1938. On April 2nd the coroner's jury committed her to stand trial for murder and she was placed in a cell at the county jail. She was told her trial would be held by a special court within a matter of weeks. But it never was.

On the afternoon of April 21st Sheriff Thompson was visiting another prisoner and walked past Mrs Hebner's cell. He noticed that she was huddled in her blankets as though asleep. Yet something told him this was no normal sleep.

He called to her, but she did not move. He opened the door and rushed inside. Cora was dead. A small brown vial, empty of its contents, was found on a table by her bunk. So too was a suicide note.

"I did not kill Will Hebner," it read, "But I can see very plainly you fellows intend to force me into saying what you want me to say, even it isn't the truth." It went on to claim that the poison had been brought into her cell by none other than William himself. "He gave me the poison the first week I was here, in case things got too hard to bear."

"Hell can't have any tortures I have not already been through," it went on. "I am giving up my life in order that all this torture may cease. I'll be seeing you before the Supreme Judge. Adios."

In accordance with her last request, Cora Hebner's body was cremated. The service was a simple one. None of her old lovers were informed.

45
THE SPURNED LOVER

Percy Brownsea was home from the war and determined to revive his old romance. He knew it wouldn't be easy, not least because he was certain that Beatrice's baby boy wasn't his. But he would make a go of it all the same. After all, he had loved Beatrice Sheen for a good many years.

It was not to be, however. It was only a matter of weeks before the couple had a flaming row. It culminated in Beatrice taking the engagement ring from her finger and throwing it at him.

"I can't stand this bickering any longer," she sobbed, "You and I are finished for good. Here's your ring, take it back."

"You can keep it, I don't want it," Brownsea told her.

"Neither do I want the bloody ring," Beatrice shouted back.

"Well, sell it then," he yelled, turning his back on her and storming off.

Percy regretted it straight away. Truth to tell, he was still besotted by the girl and would have done anything to have her back. He was an unambitious soul who, despite his adventures in the war, had no real vision beyond the boundaries of the small Dorset village in which he lived. Beatrice Sheen was the local belle and he could see no further. But she could.

Beatrice tried to avoid him, but Brownsea made it his business to be wherever she was, continually meeting her "by chance" in the street, or bumping into her "by accident" in the pub. Beatrice saw through him immediately.

"There's no use in you going on and on, Percy Brownsea," Beatrice snapped. "You and me are finished for good."

"Never, Bea," he said as he tried to make her see sense. "We've known each other too long. We've shared too much."

"We won't be sharing anything from now on," she said. "I've told you. It's over."

"You'll be back with me, Bea. You'll be back if only because you won't find another man around here."

"Don't you be so sure," she warned him.

But Percy was sure. At least he thought he was.

When Percy Brownsea first heard that Beatrice was dating Hughie Jones he was devastated. Not only did he regard Hughie as a good friend, he was also Beatrice's cousin. But he tried not to let his feelings show. When he heard that they were to be married on New Year's Day, however, he decided that positive action was called for.

How would Hughie react, Brownsea asked himself, if he revealed to him the true extent of the passion he and Beatrice had shared? It wouldn't be hard to reveal. Leafing through a stack of past love letters from Beatrice, he quickly found an explicit one. Reading it even now made him blush. Should he send it on to Hughie? "Yes," he said to himself and he began to pen a covering note. It says something of Brownsea's state of mind that he decided to make it anonymous. He signed it "From a Friend."

In the event, however, with this particular missive Brownsea lost his nerve at the last minute. It was never sent. But his nerve did not fail him with the bolder letter that he wrote on the morning of December 28th, 1956. He signed this one and he dropped it into the pillar-box without a moment's hesitation. But Hughie Jones would never receive it.

It was on the evening of December 28th that Brownsea, Beatrice and Hughie Jones found themselves having drinks together in the local pub. The evening was surprisingly jovial and everyone seemed to be having a good time.

"I'm surprised that Percy was so friendly with you this evening," remarked Beatrice after they had left.

"Why shouldn't he be?" asked Hughie in surprise.

"I thought that was obvious. I was engaged to him and now I'm going to marry you."

"Nonsense. Percy's a good sensible bloke. He knows that you and him were all washed up before I came on the scene."

"I don't think he saw it that way," Beatrice responded, but she didn't pursue it further.

Beatrice and Hughie returned to her parents' house a little after 11 o'clock. Everyone else was in bed, so the time held a special promise for them both. Beatrice was quick to clear the supper things away and get ready to go to bed. But, before she had finished the dog started barking furiously.

"What the hell is going on?" she said.

The dog continued barking, running this way and that. Something was evidently disturbing the animal.

"I'll go outside and take a look around," declared Hughie.

"Well, hurry back," Beatrice urged.

Hughie wasn't out long. Soon he had returned, but he had nothing to report.

"God knows what the dog thought he heard," he said, lowering himself on to the sofa, "there's nothing out there."

Beatrice was standing near to him and he reached out to take her hand, gently pulling her beside him.

231

As they were about to kiss there was an ear-splitting explosion and the window behind them shattered. Something stung Beatrice's face, then Hughie fell forward.

"Oh dear, Bea," he murmured.

These were the last words Hughie Jones was ever to speak. Sixty-six pellets from the shotgun had slammed into his face and neck, transforming his handsome features into a bloody mess. Beatrice knelt over him, unmindful of the nine pellets that peppered her own face.

It didn't take long for the police to realize that Percy Brownsea was the obvious suspect and he was arrested early the next morning.

He later appeared at Winchester Assizes on a charge of murder.

To begin with the prosecution thought they had an open-and-shut case. As the trial proceeded, however, it became clear that the murder charge was not going to stick. Brownsea admitted the shooting, but insisted that he had fired the gun only to shock, not to harm or kill. It was a hard point to disprove, particularly when a prosecution witness, a gun expert, demonstrated that the shotgun Brownsea had used persistently fired its pellets low. This entirely corroborated his claim that he had fired above and not at the heads of the couple.

The jury were also taken with Brownsea's appearance. He didn't look like a villain. He looked exactly what he was, an amiable and likeable, if rather simple, fellow.

After 44 minutes they returned their verdict.

"We find the prisoner not guilty of murder, but guilty of manslaughter," the foreman announced, to a faint ripple of applause. The judge, nodding agreement, sentenced Brownsea to seven years' imprisonment.

46
THE SUDDEN DEATH OF
JEALOUS JULIA

Julia Wilkins liked to surround herself with handsome animals. Her household included a male and female collie, a parrot, a monkey, three Persian cats and a robust, bewhiskered husband, Dr Walter Wilkins.

Their home was a substantial three-storey building on East Olive Street in Long Beach, Long Island. It was a nine-room residence. It was also a mess.

Julia was a wealthy woman but she refused to have help in the house. Maids, she thought, might turn her husband's head and it would be silly to put temptation in his path. He might be elderly and retired but he still had a healthy libido. "My dear old bull," she used to call him.

At 9 o'clock on the bitter cold evening of February 27th, 1919, Julia and Walter Wilkins were seen alighting in Long Beach from the New York train. The doctor's mutton-chop whiskers were almost entirely concealed by a heavy muffler and both of Julia Wilkins's chins were tucked out of sight. Still, the doctor and his wife were easily recognised, for both of them were big, strapping figures, striding their way along the street that night.

It was about half an hour later that the Long Beach police station received Dr Wilkins's frenzied phone call.

"Quick, come and help," he bellowed. "They've tried

233

to kill her, they've tried to kill my wife."

A short while later the police officers were gazing at the bloody face of Mrs Wilkins. She had sustained twenty-six vicious blows to her head, each delivered with a heavy hammer.

Dr Wilkins told the police that they had come home to be accosted by three thieves. They had beaten him and robbed him of his watch and tie-pin. They had then set upon his wife.

Had the doctor not been so respectable, the detectives might have suspected straight away. As it was, more than two weeks passed before they began to see the obvious inadequacies in his story.

There had been a fight in the house. So why had nothing been broken? Then there was the robbery. Why did the thieves settle for such a paltry haul? As it was, a search of the house quickly uncovered the supposedly stolen items. They were hidden in the springs of the sofa.

When Dr Wilkins was arrested he loudly protested his innocence, and he continued to do so all through his trial. But it was to no avail. On June 15th, 1919, he was convicted of first-degree murder and sentenced to die.

Wilkins should have been hanged at Sing Sing. But on the morning of June 29th his body was found hanging at the end of a short rope attached to a water pipe in the washroom of the Mineola jail where he was being held.

In his suicide note he declared: "Rather than be driven across the State of New York and delivered up to Sing Sing Prison, I prefer to be my own executioner."

"I am absolutely innocent of this crime," the note went on. "I dearly loved and cherished my good wife, Julia. Let her be my judge."

47

A DOOMED AFFAIR

Jean Harris met Dr Herman Tarnower at a Manhattan dinner party in 1966. Both were successful, intelligent and highly ambitious individuals, and the attraction between them was immediate. Neither was young any more. She was forty-two, he was fifty-six, and at first it seemed highly likely that the two would settle down together. Indeed, in the early months of their courtship, the idea of marriage was high on the agenda. For one reason or another, however, they never quite made it down the aisle.

Nevertheless, in the years that followed, Jean and Herman were a more or less permanent couple. As their careers progressed, geography tended to separate them. But they spent their weekends together, usually in a hotel in New York, and would holiday with each other whenever the opportunity arose.

Jean, who graduated *magna cum laude* from Smith College in 1945, was appointed headmistress of a private school in 1971. She moved again, in 1977, to become headmistress of the exclusive Madeira School for girls in McLean, Virginia. But whilst her pupils, her fellow-teachers and her employers all regarded her as a model of self-control and propriety, she still returned to New York whenever she could, and her liaison with

Dr Tarnower continued.

But it wasn't just passion and romance that kept the two together. There was also work. Herman Tarnower was writing a book, *The Scarsdale Diet*, and Jean's help in its preparation was incalculable. When it was published in 1979, and became a huge bestseller, she could rightly take a good deal of the credit.

Unfortunately, by then, however, their romance was on the wane.

Jean had always known that Dr Tarnower valued his freedom and she had suspected for some time that there were other women in his life. In particular there was Lynne Tryfoss, an attractive divorcée who was twenty-two years the doctor's junior and eight years younger than Jean. Lynne Tryfoss didn't just have youth and beauty on her side. She worked in Dr Tarnower's practice in Scarsdale, New York, so had the huge additional advantage of being almost always by his side. But even when she wasn't with him she still posed a threat. When Jean and Herman were together, away on holiday or in New York, Lynne still made her presence felt. There would be phone calls and letters. On one memorable occasion there was even a message in the personal columns of the newspaper.

Jean Harris managed to tolerate this situation fairly well. In the spring of 1980, however, she snapped. Why she did so is not known. It may have been the stress of having *The Scarsdale Diet* published. There were also problems at the Madeira School, which may have been a factor. It has also been argued that the methamphetamines that Jean had been taking from years, on prescription from Dr Tarnower, had finally disturbed the balance of her mind. In any event, Jean Harris cracked.

On March 9th she wrote a ten-page letter to Herman, voicing her feelings of rejection and humiliation. She attacked her rival for being a "vicious and psychotic whore" and listed a whole litany of complaints and grievances.

The following day, Jean finalised her will and then set off from Virginia on the five-hour drive to Tarnower's home. She arrived just before 11 o'clock and went upstairs to the doctor's bedroom. She carried in her bag a .32 calibre handgun.

Perhaps she expected to see her rival there, face to face. If she did she would have been disappointed. Lynne Tryfoss was not in the room. But there was ample evidence of her existence. The woman's underclothes lay scattered all around.

Tarnower tried to calm her. He could see she was close to hysterics. But there was really very little he could do. Jean fired four shots at her lover and he slumped to the floor.

The housekeeper heard the shots and saw Jean Harris drive away. But Harris did not try too hard to flee. As soon as she saw a police patrolman driving towards the house she did a U-turn and gave herself up. "I did it," she said simply.

Jean Harris readily admitted firing the gun, but she claimed that the killing was accidental. Her story was that she had driven to the doctor's house with the intention of killing herself. She had actually put the gun to her head and was about to pull the trigger. Tarnower had tried to pull the gun away from her, and in the tussle that followed it went off and the bullet lodged in his stomach. How this could have happened not once but four times was never explained. But Jean stuck to her story to the end.

Her trial began in November 1980. She was charged with second-degree murder and the case appeared fairly clear-cut. But as her story was revealed and evidence concerning Tarnower's amorous lifestyle was presented to the court, sympathy swayed overwhelmingly in her favour. The jury were torn between justice and the law. In the end they took eight full days before finally returning their verdict of guilty.

Sentence was passed on March 29th, 1981. Jean Harris was to spend 15 years to life in prison.

Mrs Harris listened to the sentence without displaying any emotion and has since continued to show an extraordinary strength of character.

She is currently serving her time at the Bedford Hills Correctional Facility. She campaigns for prison reform and also uses her skills to teach inmates and help their prospects of employment when they are released.

Her book about her prison experience, *They Always Call Us Ladies*, was published in 1988.

48
MURDER AT THE SAVOY

Prince Ali Kemal Fahmy Bey was barely out of his teens, but he was old enough to fall in love. He did this with a vengeance in 1922, and the consequences were disastrous.

The object of Prince Fahmy's affection was a Parisian beauty, Marguerite Laurent. Ten years his senior, Marguerite had only just divorced her first husband when they met, and she accepted the Prince's attentions with alacrity. In no time they were lovers and, soon enough, talk of marriage was in the air. By the end of the year Marguerite had converted to Islam and everything was ready for the ceremony. In December 1922 the wedding took place.

Alas, however, the cultural divide between the Egyptian playboy and his French paramour extended well beyond religion. Prince Fahmy expected his women to be obedient and dutiful, whereas Marguerite had no such notion. She was imperious and self-assured and not in the least used to being bossed around. The couple had no end of violent clashes. "With women," declared the prince after locking his wife in her room for 24 hours, "one must act with energy and be severe." Needless to say, Marguerite was not impressed with this attitude. But she was a forthright woman and gave as good as she got.

Within a month of their wedding the pattern was set for
how their marriage would be. Not a day went by without a
fight or an argument, and often as not it ended in slaps and
punches. And the couple were not ashamed to conduct
their rows in public. Soon their reputation for arguments
was known to almost every member of polite society in
Paris, Cairo and London.

It was in the spring of 1923, when they were in London, that the Fahmys' mutual animosity reached its climax. They had come to the city ostensibly because Marguerite needed some minor surgery and had chosen a
London hospital to attend to her needs. But listening to
their screams in the restaurant of their hotel few people
would have guessed that the French lady's health was
anything but robust.

They were staying at the Savoy Hotel on the Strand
and during the course of the evening they began yet
another heated argument. Over dinner in the hotel's el-
egant restaurant they began shouting at each other. The
princess was heard to say: "You shut up or I'll smash
this bottle over your head." The prince's reply was not
recorded, but one can guess what it was.

Later, as the band began to play, the band-leader
invited Marguerite to choose a tune. She stared at him
fixedly. "I don't want to hear any music tonight; my
husband's just threatened to kill me," she screeched.

Trying to make light of the situation, the maestro
turned to the lady and smiled: "Well, I hope you live
through the night."

At about 2 o'clock the following morning a porter saw
Prince Fahmy come out of his luxury suite and walk into
the corridor. He was dressed in his pyjamas. Moments
later his wife came out too, still in her evening dress. She
shouted something at the porter but it was in French
and he was unable to understand her. But he did know
that she was in danger of waking the other guests in the
hotel and requested that they both return to their rooms.

The porter turned to walk away. A few moments later three shots rang out. The porter ran back to their suite and saw Prince Fahmy. He was lying on the floor between the twin beds and bleeding profusely. Marguerite Fahmy was beside him holding a gun.

A few hours later the prince died and his wife was taken into custody.

The trial of Mme Fahmy opened on July 23rd 1923. It was, to say the least, not an exercise in race relations. Every prejudice that could be raised against the Egyptian was raised. Madame Fahmy, by contrast, was presented as a model of decorum, culture and civilization. "Members of the jury," announced her advocate in his closing speech, "I want you to open the doors so this Western woman can go out," thus summarizing, quite neatly, the whole mood of the trial.

Mme Fahmy insisted that the gun had gone off entirely by accident. She was terrified and clutching the weapon in panic. When the thing exploded in her hand she had no idea what had happened. How this "accident" managed to happen no less than three times in close succession, each time the bullet landing conveniently in her husband's head and chest, was never explained.

Marguerite's advocate made a great deal of her husband's supposed sexual predilections. The court heard that Prince Fahmy was a sadist and a bully. Mme Fahmy made explicit references to her husband's perverted sexual practices and also his taste for violence. That night, she said, he had seized her by the throat and once more threatened to kill her. There was also a strong implication that her husband's sexual preferences were deviant in the extreme.

Mme Fahmy's case was helped by the testimony of Prince Fahmy's secretary, Said Ernani, who though denying his master was violent by nature did admit that the prince had once hit his wife so forcefully that he dislocated her jaw. That Ernani was not entirely critical of his master was explained away by innuendo. It was rumoured that he and Fahmy enjoyed a homosexual relationship.

The prosecution tried to bring some balance to the proceedings by drawing attention to Marguerite Fahmy's own history and her own sexual inclinations. The judge, however, refused to admit this evidence. It would, he believed, prejudice the jury against her. These revelations, therefore, were never heard.

The jury took less than an hour to acquit Mme Fahmy. The princess, who had been portrayed throughout the proceedings as the innocent and abused wife of a cruel and distasteful husband, walked free.

Madame Fahmy went on to become a minor film star. "It's terrible to have killed Ali," she said, "but I spoke the truth."

49

CONVENT OF LUST AND MURDER

It was an unlikely love affair. He was a bullying aristocrat, she was a nun. But in the last years of the sixteenth century a romance of a sort developed between them. To begin with it was simply a case of the couple holding hands, but in no time at all Gian Paolo Osio was spending his nights at the convent of Santa Margherita, often as not in the bed of Sister Virginia de Leyva.

Of course, this could not have been done without the complicity of others. All Osio's servants knew of their master's affair with Sister Virginia. So too did many of the tradesman in the Italian town of Monza in Lombardy. Father Paolo Arrigone, a priest from the nearby church of San Maurizio, helped the couple's romance develop and even Sister Virginia's fellow-nuns at the convent had their part to play.

Sisters Ottavia, Candida, Benedetta and Silvia aided Sister Virginia by admitting Osio to their convent and keeping a lookout whilst the lovemaking was taking place, nd soon they played an even more significant role in the affair. After a while Osio invited the Sisters into the bedroom to watch, and from there it was a logical progression to orgies involving Osio and all five Sisters, and this eventually became a regular occurrence. Sister Virginia and her four helpers became totally corrupted. After Osio introduced Sister Candida to Father Arrigone, another liaison was formed. At a future court hearing, the nun would testify that she visited the priest in his church and, through the grille in the Parlatory door, "touched his shameful parts".

The local apothecary, Raneiro Roncino, also gave assistance. He supplied Sister Virginia with a constant supply of contraceptive potions. What Roncino put into these potions is not known. But one thing is known: they didn't work. In 1601 Sister Virginia became pregnant, and early in 1602 she gave birth to a stillborn boy.

Comparatively few people knew about the pregnancy and the lovers wanted to keep it that way. Osio dealt with the disposal of the body and he visited the convent every night in order to drink the milk from Sister Virginia's breasts. Their affair continued.

Inevitably, Sister Virginia became pregnant again. In August, 1604, she gave birth to a girl. By now, however, many of the nuns in the convent had grown tired of her antics, and though the baby was cared for by nuns still loyal to Sister Virginia, a spirit of rebellion was openly brewing. Previously threats of violence from Osio and his friends had kept the recalcitrant nuns in order but the movement against Sister Virginia was gaining ground.

Sister Caterina, a young novice, decided to resort to blackmail. The Bishop was due to pay a visit from Milan, and she threatened to tell him all that had been going on. In an attempt to quieten her. Caterina was locked up in solitary confinement. Sister Virginia spent hours trying to reason with her, but Caterina was adamant.

There was only one thing to do. On the night of July 28th, 1606, as Sister Virginia kept a lookout, Osio entered Caterina's cell and smashed in the novice's head with a woolwinder taken from the convent workshop. Her body was put in a sack and in the early hours of the morning taken through the streets of Monza to Osio's house, where it was disposed of.

But there was a witness. The town's blacksmith, Signor Ferrari, had seen the body being carried from the convent to Osio's house and he started dropping broad hints to that effect. Osio acted quickly, A few days after Caterina's murder, Ferrari's lifeless body was found near his forge. He had been stabbed about 70 times.

The lesson of Ferrari's murder was lost on Roncino, the apothecary. He also started talking too freely about the potions he had made for "someone at the convent who had some connection with a member of the local aristocracy". One night as he walked home from his shop, he was cut down by a hail of shots. Yet, though badly injured, Roncino survived.

The local authorities sent a report on the murder of Ferrari and the attempted murder of Roncino to the Governor of Milan, Don Pedro Enriquez Acevedo. Osio's name appeared in the report as being a prime suspect in both cases. The Governor, however, moved warily. After all, he was up against some of the most influential people in the land.

In the event, he acted quite shrewdly, for he had Osio arrested and taken to Pavia Castle, without having any specific charges levelled against him.

As Don Pedro had anticipated, his action caused rumours about Osio and the convent of Santa Margherita to become rife. Eventually, the gossip reached the Vatican, and from there an instruction was sent to Cardinal Federico Borromeo, Milan's leading ecclesiastical authority, to conduct an inquiry into the goings-on at the convent.

The Cardinal first questioned Sister Virginia, who admitted her liaison with Osio, without actually going into details of her two pregnancies or the murder of Sister Caterina. In her defence Sister Virginia said that she had been forced to enter the convent at the age of 14. She was therefore not a "true nun" and could not be guilty of sacrilege.

Cardinal Borromeo, renowned for his liberal views on the question of "forced" religious vows, decided to treat Sister Virginia leniently. She was ordered to do penance and to promise never to see Osio again.

In October, 1607, Osio escaped from Pavia Castle. Unfortunately, his time in prison had taught him nothing. Instead of going into hiding, he returned to Monza. He was bent on completing his unfinished business with Roncino. In broad daylight, and in front of several witnesses, he walked into the apothecary's shop, drew a dagger and stabbed Roncino to death.

There was a huge public outcry. A mob besieged Father Arrigone in his church. Eventually the priest managed to sneak out and, fearing for his life, fled to Milan. The Governor of Milan requested the Pope to launch a full inquiry into the convent of Santa Margherita. Sister Virginia then made the worst possible decision. She allowed Osio sanctuary in the convent.

Immediately the Prioress, Sister Angela, informed Cardinal Borromeo. The liberal-minded cleric must have felt a tinge of sadness as he ordered soldiers into the convent to remove Sister Virginia. But this fallen nun was not going to give in easily. As soldiers burst into her bedroom she took up Osio's sword and put up a strong resistance before being overpowered and taken away.

In the next room, Osio, unarmed and disguised in a nun's habit, cowered in a corner. With the onset of darkness, he changed back into his own clothes and escaped over the back wall. But he would be back.

On December 22nd, 1607, Sister Virginia poured out the whole sordid story to a court headed by the Very Reverend Gerolamo Saraceno, Vicar of the Archdiocesan Court of Milan. The court listened in shocked silence, a silence that continued as others, including Sisters Ottavia, Candida, Benedetta and Silvia, gave their evidence. It was all too much for Sister Ottavia. On the third day of her interrogation she died.

After two weeks the hearing was finished. Everyone in court had been totally unprepared for what they had heard. The Very Reverend Saraceno commented that Satan himself had taken up residence in the convent.

For the next few months Sister Virginia languished in prison while her fate was being decided. Also in prison awaiting sentence were her three remaining accomplices, along with Father Arrigone, whose arrest in Milan demonstrated how thorough the inquiry into the events at Santa Margherita had been.

On October 18th, 1608 all five were taken to Milan to hear their sentences. Sister Virginia was dealt with first. She collapsed as her sentence was read out: "You are condemned to the punishment and penance of perpetual imprisonment in the convent of Santa Valeria, in Milan. There you shall be shut into a small cell, whose door shall be blocked by a wall of plaster and stones. You shall remain there so long as you shall live, enclosed and walled up until your death. In the wall of the cell, only a small hole shall be left through which food and other necessary things may be passed, so that you do not die of hunger."

The same sentence was passed on Sisters Benedetta, Candida and Silvia. Father Arrigone was sent to the galleys for two years and banished from Monza for ever.

Meanwhile, Osio was still free. With a price on his head, he had been forced to live rough for almost a year. At last, unable to stand it any longer, he went to the home of an old friend, Count Lodovico Taverna, to beg for help. Taverna refused to listen. Instead he took him prisoner, locked him in the dungeon, then sent for a priest.

Under torture, Osio confessed everything. When he had finished, Taverna took the priest to one side and whispered something to him. As the priest left the cell, Taverna took out a knife and cut Osio's throat. His head was cut off, stuck on a pole and exhibited in the main square at Monza. The Count also sent for the Governor of Milan.

On arrival the Governor formally identified Osio's head. He then removed it from the pole and trod it into the ground, muttering: "The young lion and the dragon shalt thou tread under thy feet."

The years passed, yet though her accomplices died, Sister Virginia lived on. For 14 years she survived her living hell. She never had a change of clothes and no attempt was made at sanitation or hygiene.

On September 25th, 1622, Cardinal Borromeo exercised compassion and ordered Sister Virginia's release. Opening up the cell proved to be a horrific task for the workmen to carry out. When the door was opened they reeled back, several vomiting violently, as the tiny room disgorged the unbearable stench generated by so many years of unsanitised human occupation.

But there was no time to recover from this shock before they were subjected to an experience of absolute terror. Stumbling towards them out of the darkness of that tomb came something barely recognisable as being of human origin.

Little more than a living skeleton, the thing shuffled forwards. One bony arm was stretched out in front of it as it felt its way along. With the other it shielded its eyes from the light. Although she weighed very little, her spindly legs could barely carry her along. A few strands of dank white hair hung from her skull, but for the most part her head was bald. Her face was horribly wrinkled, her mouth completely devoid of teeth. She looked about 100 years old.

In reality Sister Virginia was 46 years of age when she was released and no one really expected her to survive. But slowly her strength returned. And, despite her ordeal, she had lost none of her faculties. Eventually the Church decided that it still had a use for her.

Right up to her death in 1651, at the age of 75, Sister Virginia was entrusted with the task of writing uplifting moral tracts for the benefit of nuns troubled by sexual temptation.

50
MURDER FOR LOVE

Much has been written about the power of love but nowhere has that power been more graphically and horribly demonstrated than in the case of Denise Labbé.

Labbé was born in the village of Melesse in the northwest corner of France in 1926. She had a difficult childhood, experiencing not only the war but also her father's suicide. But she was a bright and intelligent girl and managed to overcome her difficulties. When she was sixteen she left home and travelled to Rennes, where she found herself a job as a secretary at the National Institute of Statistics.

Denise was a lively spirit and she wasted no time discovering the highlights of the city that was now her home. In particular, she got involved with the city's student life. She had numerous affairs with young men from Rennes University, and it wasn't long before one of them made her pregnant. She thought it was probably a doctor of whom she was very fond. But it might not have been. In any case, the father's identity was entirely academic. At the tender age of eighteen, Denise had no intention of getting married.

When Catherine, her baby girl, was born, she was taken to live with Denise's mother in Blois and Denise returned to Rennes. She was now a little wiser and a little more cautious, but no less romantic.

In May 1954 Denise Labbé met twenty-four-year-old Jacques Algarron, an officer cadet at the Saint-Cyr military school and, by all accounts a brilliant mathematician. She immediately fell madly in love with him. But it was a bad choice.

For all his brilliance, Algarron had a bizarre view of the world. He was steeped in the ideas of Nietzsche, and ardently believed in the theory of the superman. Needless to say, the superman he had in mind was himself. For Jacques Algarron, he declared, normal rules and morality did not apply. He had transcended the world's petty views of right and wrong and, naturally, his partner would have to transcend them too.

Besotted by him as she was, Denise fell into line with his bizarre ideas. He dominated her completely and she willingly did his bidding. When he asked her to make love to him, she consented readily. When he asked her to make love to other men whilst he hid in the closet, she did this too. And, when he then demanded she beg his forgiveness for her infidelity, she agreed. It was a test, he said, to prove her devotion. "To merit my love, you must go from suffering to suffering."

These demands, however, were merely preludes to a far more sinister and fearful request. This came on August 29th, 1954. Algarron told her she would have to kill her own daughter. "Do this," he said, "or I will have to leave you."

Denise protested, but Algarron wouldn't be swayed. For him it was the ultimate test of her devotion. If she did it, he said, he would marry her. If she failed, then he would bid her adieu. "It takes courage to kill your own daughter," he beamed.

Despite her love for little Catherine, who was now two and a half, Denise was so completely bewitched by Jacques Algarron that she finally agreed to his horrible request.

It was not easy. Denise tried to kill her daughter a number of times, but it always ended in tears and failure.

She tried to drop the child out of the window, but lost her nerve at the last moment. Then she threw Catherine into a canal, but a passer-by rescued her. A second attempt at drowning was also thwarted when a neighbour heard the child's cries. But, on November 8th, 1954, Denise tried once more, and this time she succeeded. She drowned Catherine in the stone washbasin in her mother's home.

Initially Denise told everyone that Catherine had drowned entirely by accident. The baby had slipped whilst she was washing her, she said. But friends were suspicious, and the police were brought in.

After being questioned about the accident, Denise finally admitted the truth. "Yes, I killed my daughter but it was a ritual murder." She then told them the whole story.

After the traumatic experience of seeing her child dead and then being arrested for the killing, Denise's passion for Algarron quickly ebbed. She now saw him for the monster he was. To the Rennes police she described him as a "cultist devil" and spared no details of his extraordinary behaviour.

Jacques Algarron was promptly arrested and the pair were jointly charged with murder.

Their trial began at the Loiret-Cher Assizes in Blois in May 1955. Labbé expressed her sorrow and guilt, Algarron remained impassive. The jury were out for nearly three hours to deliberate their verdict.

In the end both were found guilty but the jury decided that, in the case of Denise Labbé there were extenuating circumstances. She was under the "spell" of her lover, they said, and should be treated with mercy.

Labbé was sentenced to life imprisonment. Jacques Algarron to 20 years' hard labour.

INDEX OF VILLAINS

TRUE CRIME LIBRARY SERIES

A DATE WITH THE HANGMAN
T.J. Leech
£4.99

This is an outstanding volume of British murder cases,
uncanny and strange. The killers are an odd mix –
robbers and rapists, cop-killers and conmen, jealous
lovers, paedophiles, madmen and ruthless women.
But all had one thing in common ... a date with
the hangman.

MURDER WITH VENOM
Brian Marriner
£4.99

A compelling study of poisons and poisoners by one of
the most outstanding crime writers of today. Sixteen
celebrated murder cases coupled with an absorbing
study of poisons and their uses makes this book a
modern classic of criminology.

BRITAIN'S GODFATHER
Edward T. Hart
£4.99

This is the story of perhaps the most remarkable man in
the annals of British organised crime. At the zenith of his
power, Darby Sabini had 300 armed men under his
command. With judges, politicians and senior policemen
in his pay he created the most lucrative secret criminal
empire ever seen in Britain.

A CENTURY OF SEX KILLERS
Brian Marriner
£5.99

This book confirms Brian Marriner as the leading
authority in his field. From Jack the Ripper to the Serial
Killers, the most comprehensive work available on sex
murders.

ON DEATH ROW*and* WOMEN ON DEATH ROW
Mike James
£4.99

Two absorbing studies of those who have lived on Death
Row, and the interminable anguish of their existence on
Death Row, knowing that the next day could be their
last.

FATAL ATTRACTION
Mike James
£4.99

Tenderness turned to rage, infatuation to obsession,
domination to subjugation - each of these twenty
incredible stories are of love becoming a terrifying
mania.

BEDSIDE BOOK OF MURDER
Mike James
£4.99

Fifty gripping stories selected from the celebrated
archives of the True Crime Library.